# THIRD GRADE

## TIMBERDOODLE'S
## CURRICULUM HANDBOOK

### 2020-2021 EDITION

"EIFFEL" COVER DOODLE BY MEGHAN, AGE 13
"MOBI MATH" COVER DOODLE BY EMMA, AGE 15
ALL THE AMAZING INTERIOR DOODLES PROVIDED BY OUR TALENTED CUSTOMERS

# Welcome to Third Grade

# WE'RE SO GLAD YOU'RE HERE!

Congratulations on choosing to homeschool this year! Whether this is your first year as a teacher or your tenth, we're confident you'll find that there is very little that compares to watching your child's learning take off. In fact, teaching can be quite addictive, so be forewarned!

## ON YOUR MARK, GET SET, GO!

Preparing for your first "school day" is very easy. Peruse this guide, look over the typical schedule, browse the introductions in your books, and you will be ready to go.

## GET SUPPORT

Are you looking for a place to hang out online with like-minded homeschoolers? Do you wonder how someone else handled a particular science experiment? Or do you wish you could encourage someone who is just getting started this year? Join one or more of our Facebook groups.

**Timberdoodlers of all ages:**
https://www.facebook.com/groups/Timberdoodle/

**Timberdoodlers with 1st- through 4th-grade students:**
www.facebook.com/groups/ElementaryTimberdoodle

## SCHEDULE CUSTOMIZER

Your 2020–2021 Third-Grade Curriculum Kit includes access to our Schedule Customizer where you can not only adjust the school weeks but also tweak the checklist to include exactly what you want on your schedule. To get started, just click the link in your access email and visit the scheduling website!

**www.TimberdoodleSchedules.com**

If you ordered through a charter school or don't have that link for some other reason, just email schedules@Timberdoodle.com and we'll get that sorted out ASAP. (Including your order number will really speed that process up for you.)

## WE WILL HELP

We would love to assist you if questions come up, so please don't hesitate to contact us with any questions, comments, or concerns. Whether you contact us by phone, email, or live online chat, you will get a real person who is eager to serve you and your family.

## YOU WILL LOVE THIS!

This year you and your student will learn more than you hoped while having a blast. Ready? Have an absolutely amazing year!

# CONTENTS

## ITEM-BASED RESOURCES

## WHEN YOU'RE DONE HERE

# MEET YOUR HANDBOOK

**WELCOME TO YOUR TEACHING TOOLBOX!**

### Simple Is Better
We really believe that, so your guide is as simple as we could make it.

### 1. The Planning
First up are all the details on planning your year, including your annual planner and sample weekly checklists, the absolute backbones of Timberdoodle's curriculum kits. More on those in a moment.

### 2. Reading Challenge
Next up is the reading challenge, complete with book ideas to give you a head start.

### 3. Item-by-Item Details
We include short bios of each item in your kit, ideal for refreshing your memory on why each is included or to show off exactly what your third-grader will be covering this year. This is where we've tucked in our tips or tricks to make this year more awesome for all of you.

### 4. Teacher Resources
In this section, you'll find our favorite articles and tidbits amassed in our more-than-30 years of homeschool experience.

### 5. Items with Special Instructions
Here you'll find a week-by-week schedule for Mosdos.

### 6. Book Suggestions
Finally, we'll conclude with specific book ideas for your reading challenge this year.

### All the Details Included
This Timberdoodle curriculum kit is available in three different standard levels: Basic, Complete, or Elite. This allows you to choose the assortment best suited to your child's interest level, your family's schedule, and your budget. In this guide, you'll find an overview and any tips for each of the items included in the Elite Curriculum Kit. If you purchased a Basic or Complete kit, or if you customized your kit, you chose not to receive every item, so you'll only need to familiarize yourself with the ones which were included in your kit.

### Don't Panic, You Didn't Order Too Much Stuff!
We know you. OK, maybe not you personally, but we have yet to meet a homeschooler who doesn't have other irons in the fire. From homesteading or running a business to swimming lessons or doctor appointments, your weeks are not dull. As you unpack your box, you may be asking yourself how you'll ever fit it all in.

We'll go in-depth on schedules momentarily, but for now know that most of the items in your kit feature short lessons, not all of them should be done every day, and your checklist is going to make this incredibly manageable. Really!

# TIPS & TRICKS

## YOUR FIRST WEEK, STATE LAWS, AND MORE

### Week 1 Hints

As you get started this year, realize that you are just getting your sea legs. Expect your studies to take a little longer and be a little less smooth than they will be by the end of the year. As you get your feet under you, you will discover the rhythm that works best for you! If you don't know where to begin each day, why not try starting with something from the Thinking Skills category? It will get your child's brain in gear and set a great tone for the rest of the day.

### Find Your Pace

We asked parents who used this kit how long their students spent on "school." Most said that they spent 2-5 hours per day. That is a wide variation, so make sure you allow yourself and your child some time to find your own rhythm!

### Books First, or Not?

Some goal-oriented students might like to start each day with bookwork and end with fun, hands-on time. Others might prefer to intersperse the hands-on thinking games, STEM, and so forth, between more intensive subjects to give their brains a clean slate.

### A Little Every Day, or All at Once?

Depending on your preferences, your child's attention span, and what other time commitments you have (teaching other children, doctor appointments, working around a baby's nap), there are many different ways to schedule your week. Some families like to do a little portion from nearly all subjects every day, while others prefer to blast out an entire week's work within a subject in a single sitting. Throughout the year, you can tinker around with your daily scheduling and see what approach works best for your family.

### Tips for Newbies

If you're new to homeschooling, it might be helpful for you to know that some subjects are typically taught and practiced several times a week for the best mastery. These would include basic math instruction, phonics, and spelling. However, more topical subjects such as geography, history, and science are often taught all at once. Meanwhile, thinking skills, STEM, and art, plus hands-on learning and games, can be even more tailored to the preferences of the child or used for independent learning while you are busy.

## What About the Courses Which You Don't Work on Every Week?

As you go over your checklist, you'll notice that some of your courses are "2-3 a month" or "as desired", and that may leave you confused on how to tackle them. Here are a few options: You could go ahead and do it every week, completing the course early. You could set aside the item for summer (see below). Or you could complete it as directed, of course!

## The Summer Plan

If you're looking at all these tools and feeling a little overwhelmed, or if you just wish you had more structured activities for the summer, feel free to grab a handful of items from the kit and set them aside for summer. Then, set a reminder on your phone or calendar to remind you which ones they are and where you stashed them so you won't forget to use them!

*Continued on the next page.*

# TIPS & TRICKS, CONT.

### Meeting State Requirements

Check https://www.hslda.org/laws to see the most current information on your specific requirements. For many states, it is sufficient to hang on to your completed and dated weekly checklists along with a sampling of your child's best work this year. Some states ask you to add in a state-specific topic or two, such as Vermont history, or a generic course like P.E. or health. We have a summary on our blog comparing your kit to state requirements, but HSLDA is the gold standard for current legal information.

### P.E.? Health?

We suggest thinking outside the box on this. Many of the science courses have a health component that meets the requirement. P.E. is a great way to fit your child's favorite activity into the school schedule. Ballet, soccer, horseback riding, swimming... there are so many fun ways to check off P.E. this year!

### Put Your Child in Charge?

The weekly checklists are the framework of your week, designed for maximum flexibility. Just check off each item as you get it done for the week and you'll be able to see at a glance that you still need to do ____ this week. (This is true of the daily checklists, as well–just on a shorter schedule.) Many students even prefer to get all their work done early in the week and enjoy all their leisure time at once!

## Do Hard Things and Easy Ones

Our family provides foster care for kids who need a safe place for a while. This has exposed us to a whole new world of hard days and stressful weeks. If your child is struggling today, you are not failing if you take a step back and have him start with his most calming project. For our crew, often that would be art or the reading challenge. You even have a little slush room in most subjects, so don't hesitate to trim the lessons short on a busy or challenging week or pause schoolwork today for a complete reset and tackle it fresh tomorrow.

At the same time, you are not doing your child any favors if you never teach him how to work through a challenge. After all, you have hard days as a parent and still get up, drink your coffee, and jump back in. Be aware of your own tendency to have your child either buckle down and push through or ease off completely, then work to provide a healthy balance for your child, particularly if he is in the process of healing.

### Pro Tip

When you first get out a week's checklist, go ahead and check off all the things you don't need to do this week. For instance, if your child did a few extra pages of math last week or you are putting off all art kits until winter, check those off. Doesn't that feel better?

### The Sample Schedules

We're including a sample annual planner on page 19, followed by sample weekly planners for each level of your kit, reflecting a typical 36-week school year. This lets you see at a glance how this might work for you, even before you get a moment to sit down at your computer and print your own custom-fitted schedule.

# ASK YOUR THIRD-GRADER!

## A JUST-FOR-FUN BEGINNING OF THE YEAR INTERVIEW

Jot down your child's answers here to capture a fun time capsule of his third-grade year.

1. What do you want to be when you grow up?

2. Who are some people you would like to learn something from? (Is there a particular something you want to learn?)

3. Do you want to play an instrument? If so, what kind would you choose? If more than one, list them.

4. What is your favorite food to make? To eat? That someone else makes?

5. What's the most important, longest, or most interesting thing you've memorized?

6. What is your favorite subject to learn?

7. What makes you laugh? (Or who?)

8. What activities does your family like to do (as individuals or together)?

9. What do you know about outer space/ the universe/ constellations?

10. Where is your favorite place?

11. What's something Mom (or someone else in your family) always says?

www.timberdoodle.com  •  ©2020

**A SELF-PORTRAIT (OR PHOTO) OF** _____

# MEET YOUR ONLINE SCHEDULER

## GETTING THE MOST OUT OF YOUR PLANNERS

### Use the Customizer

On the next pages you'll find sample weekly checklists for Basic, Complete, and Elite kits. Before you photocopy 36 of them, though, take a moment to check out the custom online schedule builder that came free with your kit. You'll not only easily adjust the weeks, but you'll also tweak the checklist to include exactly what you want listed. Plus, you'll be able to print your weekly checklists directly from the schedule builder so you don't have to do that by photocopying! www.TimberdoodleSchedules.com

### Activating Your Account

Before you can get started, you'll need your account activated for the online schedule builder. If you didn't get

an activation email (perhaps you ordered through a charter school so we don't have your email address), shoot us a quick email at schedules@Timberdoodle.com and we'll get that straightened out ASAP. Including your order number really speeds that process up, but our team is skilled at finding your activation info with whatever order data you have.

### What's Your Dream Schedule?

Now that you're ready you'll want to know two things:

### 1. How Many Weeks Do You Want to Do School?

A standard school year is 36 weeks + breaks. Some families prefer to expedite and complete the entire year in fewer weeks–a great option for those of you who'd like to get all this year's school done before baby arrives, for instance. Or perhaps your family, like ours, prefers to school year-round and keep that brain sharp.

### 2. What Breaks Do You Want?

Thanksgiving, Christmas, winter break, spring break... you could also add in weeks off that you're traveling, have guests, baby is coming, or...

Typically you'll be adding full-week

breaks only, so unless you're traveling to Disneyland® for little Eloise's birthday, you don't need to add that to the calendar. For single-day breaks you'll likely prefer to just shuffle the work to earlier/later in the same week and keep on task otherwise. If you're using a daily schedule (next page), though, you may find it worth your time to enter days off, as well.

### Choosing Your Items

Now just pop that data into the online schedule and scroll down to see the items you might have in your kit. Unchecking the boxes for any items you don't have removes them from your list. You'll also see "Alternative Items" listed under each subject. This usually includes all of our most popular customizations for this grade so that you can simply check a box and switch the scheduler to an upper or lower level math, for instance.

### Add Custom Courses

Your course list is limited only by your imagination. Perhaps your friend wrote you a custom curriculum you'd like to include, your family makes up a band and you'd like to have practice on this list, or you need to list ballet since that's P.E. this year. At the very bottom of the page you'll find a place to

add in as many courses as you'd like. Just walk through the prompts on-screen to get it all set up.

### Tweak It to Perfection

Do you have everything set? On the next screen you'll have some fun options.

*Continued on the next page.*

# MEET YOUR ONLINE SCHEDULER, CONT.

### 1. Large-Font Edition
Want a large-font option? Just check the box. If you don't like how it looks you can always come back and uncheck it.

### 2. Show Dates
Check this box if it's helpful for you to see at a glance that week 17 is January 13th–17th, for instance. Some teachers find this incredibly helpful while others prefer to move breaks around on the fly, making the dates irrelevant.

### 3. Weekly or Daily?
We prefer a weekly schedule, for the simple reason that our weeks are rarely without some anomaly. Off to the dentist's Tuesday? You won't fall behind by taking a day off.

Or perhaps you have Friday Robotics Camp for a couple of weeks and need to get all the week's work done over four days instead of five. No problem! This approach also teaches time-management skills (see the article on Independent Learning at the back of this book).

However, we've heard from many of you that having a daily schedule, especially for the first month, is a real life-saver. So we developed one, and if it helps you, fantastic! The daily scheduler is programmed to split up the work as evenly as possible over the week, with the beginning of the week having any extra pages or lessons. (We all know that end-of-the-week doldrums are a real thing!)

### Moving Courses to Certain Days
If you're opting for the daily scheduler, you do have some helpful fine-tuning options. Just click "Edit" on the course

in question and you'll have the option of selecting on which days of the week the course will appear. This lets you do things like schedule history only on Wednesday because that is co-op day. Or, you could schedule science only on Tuesday or Thursday and STEM on Friday or Monday so that science and STEM are never on the same day.

### Pro Tip
You can also opt to exclude an item from certain weeks. This is useful if you already know that you want to save an art kit for May so that Grandma can do it with Eloise, or if you don't want to break out the graphic novel until after Christmas since you've set it aside as a gift.

### 4. Show Unit Range?
This feature sounds so very data-y and not super helpful, but we think you just might love it. Instead of saying that you

need to do seven pages of math this week, check this box to have it remind you that you're on worksheets 50–56 this week, for example. If you prefer extreme flexibility, leave this box unchecked. But if you're afraid of falling behind without knowing it, this box will be your hero.

### Make More Lists

If you have one student and one teacher, you may feel free to buzz past this idea. But if you have an extra teacher– perhaps your spouse, a grandparent, or even an older sibling who wants the bonding time, then this may simplify your life! Instead of putting all of your child's work on a single list, you could put all the subjects you will teach on your list and all of the remaining subjects on "Grandma's list" for her ease.

If you have twins or multiple students at the same grade level, you can also make multiple lists to meet each student's needs best.

### That's It!

Click "Generate Schedule", then "View Generated Schedule", and you're ready to print it and get started!

FYI, our scheduler is constantly being improved, so for the most current instructions please refer to the blog link in your activation email.

### Ideas Our Team Is Working On

At the time of this printing, our team is working to add a time log to these lists for those of you whose states require it. We're also adding a way to easily email the schedule to yourself for your records, adding a progress report, and fine-tuning how you add time off to your schedule. These are all features that you may expect to see more about on the afore mentioned blog post. Also, please let us know if you think of more features that our team should consider!

| | CURRICULUM | LESSONS OR PAGES | = PER WEEK |
|---|---|---|---|
| **Language Arts** | Daily 6-Trait Writing | 25 weeks | 1 week's work |
| | Mosdos Literature Opal | 36 sub-sections | 1 sub-section |
| | Spelling You See D | 36 weeks | 1 week's work |
| | CursiveLogic | 10 weeks + 14 practice pages | 1 week's work or practice page |
| | First Language Lessons 3 | 110 lessons | 3 lessons |
| | Beginning Word Roots | 27 lessons/reviews | one lesson or review |
| | The Adventures of Robin Hood | 1 book | as desired |
| **Math** | Math-U-See | 30 lessons | 1 lesson/7 worksheets |
| | Wrap-ups Multiplication | 10 boards | once a week |
| | Möbi Max | unlimited | once a week |
| | Extreme Dot-to-Dot: Baby Animals | 32 puzzles | 1 puzzle |
| **Thinking Skills** | Critical and Creative 3 | 142 pages | 4 pages |
| | Circuit Maze | 60 challenges | 1-2 challenges |
| | Anomia Kids | unlimited | once a week |
| **History & Social Studies** | The Story of the World 3 | 42 chapters | 1-2 chapters |
| | True Stories of the Revolutionary War | 1 book | as desired |
| | Skill Sharpeners Geography | 132 pages | 4 pages |
| | Famous Figures | 10 figures | 1-2 a month |
| | Puzzleball Globe | 1 puzzle | once a month |
| **Science** | Science in the Scientific Revolution | 90 lessons | 2-3 lessons |
| | Dr. Bonyfide 1 | 108 pages | 3 pages |
| **STEM** | GraviTrax Deluxe Set | 33 models | 1 model |
| | Typing Instructor for Kids | unlimited | 3 lessons |
| | Scratch Coding Cards | 75 cards | 2-3 cards a week |
| **Art** | Zentangle for Kids | 42 activities | 1-2 activities |
| | Doodle Adventures: Space Slugs | 105 pages | 3 pages |
| | Paint-by-Number Museum Series | 4 paintings | as desired |
| | Complete-A-Sketch 123 | 78 drawings | 2-3 drawings |
| **Etc.** | Test Prep | 128 pages | end of school year |

YOUR ANNUAL PLANNER

# WHAT IS A LESSON?

## ITEM BY ITEM SPECS

On pages 36–76 you'll find an overview of each item, including information about how we split up the work and why, but if you're looking for a quick reference pages to refresh your mind on what exactly "one lesson" means for any of your materials, here you go!

### Daily 6-Trait Writing
The course is split into 25 weeks of work. We suggest starting the one week's work per week pace after 11 weeks of school to allow you to ease into the year.

### Mosdos Literature
Do one week's work as found in the 30-week schedule on pages 96-99 in this handbook. (There are a few variations on page 41 to expand this to 36 weeks.)

We suggest completing the bulk of the workbook pages but skipping the writing, since you'll be covering that with Daily 6-Trait.

### Spelling You See D
There are 36 lessons, each of which includes five days of work. Two tips: Your day's lesson is complete after 10 minutes of work–your child does not need to finish the whole chunk. Also, if you're using a four-day week or don't get to all five days of work in a week, it is expected that you will still count that lesson as complete at the end of the week

and move to the next one.

### First Language Lessons
In this book, the lessons are very clearly marked. Do two to three lessons per week (three for sure if you're planning to do the optional end lessons about writing letters, oral lessons, and dictionary skills).

### Beginning Word Roots
You'll find 24 lessons clearly marked, each ranging from two to four pages long. There are also three review chapters. We suggest completing one entire lesson or review each week, knowing you'll either finish nine weeks early or have the flexibility to split a lesson nine times.

### CursiveLogic
This course is laid out in an easy-to-use 10-week course. Simply complete one week's work every week until you're done. (Each week includes three to four days of work, with multiple pages per day.) We suggest beginning your school year with this course and then using cursive where appropriate throughout the year. There are also 14 practice pages for use after completing the course. We suggest one page a week for weeks 11–24.

### The Adventures of Robin Hood
We suggest just turning your child loose with this book rather than putting it on the schedule.

## Math-U-See

You'll find 30 lessons here, each with seven worksheets. Since you'll only be completing as many of the worksheets as your child needs per lesson, and since completing one whole lesson a week keeps the instructional portions predictable, we suggest doing one lesson a week instead of a certain number of worksheets. If you use that method, know that you can spread a tricky lesson over two weeks up to six times this year without messing up your schedule.

## Wrap-ups Multiplication

Unlimited. We suggest having your child do it once a week, racing his previous time, until it becomes too easy for him.

## Möbi Max

Unlimited. We suggest at least one or two games a week.

## Extreme Dot-to-Dot

You'll want to do about one puzzle a week.

## Critical and Creative

While you could split this by pages (four a week), instead we suggest completing one to two units a week so that you don't lose the continuity and fun of doing all the pages on a certain topic at once.

## Circuit Maze

Just do one or two new challenges a week.

## Anomia Kids

This game is unlimited. We suggest breaking it out at least once a week and playing a few rounds.

## The Story of the World 3

With 42 chapters, you're going to want to do 3 chapters every two weeks. Or, if it's easier, just do 2 chapters one

week and 1 chapter the following week. Add in as many activities as you have the time/interest for.

## Skill Sharpeners Geography

Simply doing four pages a week will get you through this year. Keep in mind that you're free to skip the writing assignments and elaborate activities if needed, but if your student has the time and energy, these will really serve to reinforce what he's learning.

## Famous Figures of the Early Modern Era

There are 21 models to complete, each with a full-color and a color-it-yourself option. See page 59 for notes on integrating them into the most appropriate lessons.

## Puzzleball Globe

Unlimited. We suggest your child completes it once a month or so until he has it mastered.

*Continued on next page.*

# WHAT IS A LESSON? CONT.

### True Stories of the Revolutionary War
You can either time this to be used with chapter 22 of Story of the World or release it to your child at any point for free reading. It's captivating!

### Science in the Scientific Revolution
You'll see that some of the lessons in this book are color-coded red. These are optional lessons, so if you're trying to streamline your days, feel free to skip those and only do two lessons a week. If you want to do all the lessons, plan on three a week. If you ordered the Elite kit, you'll also find a printed student notebook and complete Lab Kit included for your convenience!

### Dr. Bonyfide
About three pages a week will take you through this year.

### Typing Instructor
You decide. The more time you allow, the more skills your student will gain. We'd suggest three lessons a week, but fine-tune that for your student.

### GraviTrax Deluxe
With 33 suggested models to build, we suggest 1 per week starting with the exact replication manual.

### Scratch Coding Cards
We suggest one project a week. If you're looking for a lighter approach, then try two cards a week.

### Zentangle for Kids
With 43 activities, complete 1 or 2 a week. (We didn't count gallery pages as activities, but we did count instructional spreads as well as spreads composed of pictures to tangle in and complete.)

### Doodle Adventures: Slimy Space Slugs
With 105 pages in all, your child should complete 3 a week.

### Paint-by-Number Museum Series
There are four great paintings to complete. At this age, most students will want to save these for days when they will have enough time to totally complete one. Work that in as desired.

### Complete-A-Sketch 123
You have 78 drawings to complete, and each should be done multiple times to master it. We suggest doing three for the first six weeks of school, as those are the easiest drawings. After that, just master two a week.

### Thinking Putty
Unlimited. We suggest making up at least one tin in the first week of school so that your child has a fidget handy.

### Test Prep
We usually save this for the end of the year to refresh the student on all the skills he'll need for annual testing. You won't find this on your schedule unless you add it.

| | | | | | | | | | |
|---|---|---|---|---|---|---|---|---|---|
| **Language Arts** | Daily 6-Trait Writing | 1 week's work | | | | | | | |
| | Mosdos Literature Opal | 1 sub-section | | | | | | | |
| | Spelling You See D | 1 week's work | | | | | | | |
| | CursiveLogic | 1 week's work | | | | | | | |
| **Math** | Math-U-See | 1 lesson/7 worksheets | | | | | | | |
| **Thinking Skills** | Critical and Creative 3 | 1–2 units | | | | | | | |

# WEEKLY CHECKLIST (COMPLETE)

| | | | | | | | | | |
|---|---|---|---|---|---|---|---|---|---|
| **Language Arts** | Daily 6-Trait Writing | 1 week's work | | | | | | | |
| | Mosdos Literature Opal | 1 sub-section | | | | | | | |
| | Spelling You See D | 1 week's work | | | | | | | |
| | CursiveLogic | 1 week's work | | | | | | | |
| | First Language Lessons 3 | 3 lessons | | | | | | | |
| **Math** | Math-U-See | 1 lesson/7 worksheets | | | | | | | |
| | Wrap-ups Multiplication | 1x a week | | | | | | | |
| | Möbi Max | once a week | | | | | | | |
| **Thinking Skills** | Critical and Creative 3 | 1–2 units | | | | | | | |
| | Circuit Maze | 1–2 challenges | | | | | | | |
| **History & Social Studies** | The Story of the World 3 | 1–2 chapters | | | | | | | |
| | True Stories of the Revolutionary War | as desired | | | | | | | |
| | Skill Sharpeners Geography | 4 pages | | | | | | | |
| **Science** | Science in the Scientific Revolution | 2–3 lessons | | | | | | | |
| | Dr. Bonyfide 1 | 3 pages | | | | | | | |
| **STEM** | GraviTrax | 1 model | | | | | | | |
| | Typing Instructor | 3 lessons | | | | | | | |
| **Art** | Zentangle for Kids | 1–2 activities | | | | | | | |
| | Doodle Adventures | 3 pages | | | | | | | |
| | Paint-by-Number Museum Series | as desired | | | | | | | |

www.timberdoodle.com • ©2020

| Subject | Item | Amount | | | | | |
|---|---|---|---|---|---|---|---|
| **Language Arts** | Daily 6-Trait Writing | 1 week's work | | | | | |
| | Mosdos Literature Opal | 1 sub-section | | | | | |
| | Spelling You See D | 1 week's work | | | | | |
| | CursiveLogic | 1 week's work | | | | | |
| | First Language Lessons 3 | 3 lessons | | | | | |
| | Beginning Word Roots | 1 lesson | | | | | |
| | The Adventures of Robin Hood | as desired | | | | | |
| **Math** | Math-U-See | 1 lesson/7 worksheets | | | | | |
| | Wrap-ups Multiplication | once a week | | | | | |
| | Möbi Max | once a week | | | | | |
| | Extreme Dot-to-Dot: Baby Animals | 1 puzzle | | | | | |
| **Thinking Skills** | Critical and Creative 3 | 1–2 units | | | | | |
| | Circuit Maze | 1–2 challenges | | | | | |
| | Anomia Kids | once a week | | | | | |
| **History & Social Studies** | The Story of the World 3 | 1–2 chapters | | | | | |
| | True Stories of the Revolutionary War | as desired | | | | | |
| | Skill Sharpeners Geography | 4 pages | | | | | |
| | Famous Figures | 1–2 a month | | | | | |
| | Puzzleball Globe | once a month | | | | | |
| **Science** | Science in the Scientific Revolution | 2–3 lessons | | | | | |
| | Dr. Bonyfide 1 | 3 pages | | | | | |
| **STEM** | GraviTrax | 1 model | | | | | |
| | Typing Instructor | 3 lessons | | | | | |
| | Scratch Coding Cards | 2–3 cards a week | | | | | |
| **Art** | Zentangle for Kids | 1–2 activities | | | | | |
| | Doodle Adventures | 3 pages | | | | | |
| | Paint-by-Number Museum Series | as desired | | | | | |
| | Complete-A-Sketch 123 | 2–3 drawings | | | | | |

# THE READING CHALLENGE

## BASED ON THE READING CHALLENGE FOR KIDS FROM REDEEMEDREADER.COM

The Reading Challenge for Kids will get you and your child reading a broader variety of books this year and perhaps discovering new favorites. This reading challenge is heavily adapted by us and used with permission from the fine folks at RedeemedReader.com. Check out their website for more information about this reading challenge and for great book reviews and book suggestions for your kids.

### Reading Solo and Together

At this grade level, it is likely that most of these books be titles he will read independently. However, we highly recommend keeping a read-aloud time, too, as long as it's possible. Many sources recommend that parents continue reading to their children well past the time their children become accomplished readers, and we agree!

## How It Works

On the following pages, you'll find four lists of books which you are meant to read one after another this year. Not all families will make it through all the lists, so you will need to choose a reading goal early in the year and set your pace accordingly.

The Light Reader plan has 13 books, which sets a pace of 1 book every four weeks. The majority of families can and should do at least this much.

The Avid Reader plan adds another 13 books, which increases the pace to 1 book every two weeks. This is doable for most families.

The Committed Reader plan adds a further 26 books, bringing the total to 52, or 1 book every week. By including picture books, we think that even this faster pace is not too rigorous and is suitable for enthusiastic readers with time in their schedules.

The Obsessed Reader plan doubles the total yet again, bringing it to 104 books, which sets a pace of 2 books every week. We highly recommend this challenge, but it may be too intense for families with already-packed schedules!

## Getting Started

Begin with the Light plan, which includes suggestions for 13 books. Choose those books and read them in any order, checking them off as you complete them.

Next, advance to the Avid plan, using the criteria there to choose another 13 books and read them in any order.

Then it's time to move to the Committed plan with a further 26 books, again reading them in any order.

If you have completed the Committed plan (that's 52 books so far!), you are ready to brave the Obsessed plan.

If you want to finish your books in a school year rather than in an entire calendar year, the timeline shifts a bit, so be sure to set your goal at the beginning of the year and pace yourself accordingly.

Here's the pace for a 36-week schedule:

**Light Reader: One book every two to three weeks.**

**Avid Reader: One book every week or two.**

**Committed Reader: One and a half books every week.**

**Obsessed Reader: Almost three books every week.**

## How Long Do We Count Picture Books?

I recently heard this beautiful quote from Sarah Mackenzie at the Read-Aloud Revival:

"Another thing I want to point out is picture books. As your child grows older, do not stop reading picture books. Picture books are written, often times, with more eloquent, beautiful language than chapter books or middle-grade novels so the reading level in the picture book is actually higher than it is in the novel. A beautifully written picture book is like poetry and an art gallery combined into one. So they are not less than, or they're not inferior to longer novels. The beautiful thing about picture books is because they're short, you can experience more stories this way. So if you prioritize picture books over novels when it comes to reading aloud, you will actually fill your child's memories and childhood with more stories..." (Hear the whole conversation on the Read-Aloud Revival podcast, at the beginning of episode 121.)

### But I Don't Have Any Idea Which Books to Choose!

We have your back! Beginning on page 98 you'll find hundreds of book ideas you'll love this year.

If you want more ideas, we highly recommend your local librarian, the Read-Aloud Revival podcast, and the Timberdoodle Facebook groups as excellent starting points. It's also a wonderful idea to peek at the additional reading ideas in your history or science textbooks (particularly if your child was fascinated by something his courses recently touched on).

### Will This Be Expensive?

It doesn't need to be. You can read library books and e-versions, buy used, borrow from friends, and scour your family bookshelves. Don't forget that many libraries have

free e-versions, as well. It doesn't get much more convenient than that!

### But How Do I Fit This Much Reading Into My Day?

Here are nine ideas to incorporate more reading into your family's busy schedule and unique schooling style:

### 1. Use Books of Various Lengths

A longer book than you'd usually pick may be perfect as an audio book. On the flip side, if your child will be be reading to a younger sibling or you are picking a new readaloud for the whole gang, feel free to gear the book towards the younger participants, particularly if you're short on time. Picture books allow for more stories in less time, but they don't lack at all for impact.

### 2. Assign Independent Reading

This can be done in conjunction with quiet time or simply throughout the day. Our household often uses it as a strategy to calm the hyper and soothe the sad—"I need you to go read one book (or one chapter) and then come back and we'll try again."

### 3. Quiet Time!

Does your family implement a quiet time already? Reading is a natural perk for that time. Quiet time can be as simple as setting a timer for 30 minutes (or more) and having your child relax with his favorite blanket or weighted lap pad and, of course, his book. If it's possible for you to grab a book that you've been wanting to read and embrace the same plan, you'll be modeling what an ageless wonder reading can be. Of course, if your household is filled with little ones, it may be more practical for you to use this time for feeding babies

or fixing dinner and there's no shame in that, but consider your options as you plan your year.

### 4. Sneak Reading Into Your Existing Routines
What routines are already going well for you? Could you incorporate a reading time right into your existing bedtime routine, family devotions, car time, snack time, or other routine?

### 5. Audiobooks
Incorporate audiobooks and save the designated reader some time and energy. This is a particularly spectacular move for car time, art time, puzzle time, or even to smooth over particularly grumpy mealtimes.

### 6. Put the Busy Ones to Work
Encourage quiet activities such as puzzles, this year's STEM kit, or coloring while you read aloud or play the audiobook. It can be legitimately impossible for your kinesthetic learner to sit perfectly still and listen angelically, but break out the "listening time only" tools and suddenly everyone looks forward to reading!

### 7. Brothers and Sisters
You don't have to be the only one reading to your child. Have your "big kid" read to a younger sibling as part of their school lessons. The older sibling will gain fluency as your younger one soaks up the one-on-one time. (No younger ones in your home? How about cousins, playmates, grandparents, or even the family pet?)

### 8. Grandpa, Grandma, Aunties, Oh My!
Perhaps an auntie would welcome the opportunity to have Friday evenings be read-aloud time, complete with hot cocoa and scones. Or Grandma might love the idea of hosting all of her grandchildren once a month for a giant book party—each child could bring his favorite book to share. Too far away? Grandpa could record his favorite book (any audio-recording app should work), then send the book to your child so that he can read along with Grandpa.

### 9. Get a Library Routine Going
Our family has loved reading since our toddler days, but we didn't use the library well until we settled into a simple routine. For us that involves a central location for all library books and having a designated person willing to return current books and pick up the holds each week. Those simple steps have quickly borne fruit with many more hours spent reading "new" books!

### Let's Read!
Pick your plan, choose some books with your child, and get started!

| The Challenge | The Book You Chose | Date Completed |
|---|---|---|
| 1. A book about being a Christian or about what the Bible teaches | IF THE WORLD WERE A VILLAGE | 10/16 |
| 2. A book about the world | THIS IS HOW WE DO IT | 10/20 |
| 3. A biography | ABE LINCOLN | 8/28 |
| 4. A classic novel/story | DOCTOR DOOLITTLE | 9/5 |
| 5. A book your grandparent (or other relative) says was his/her favorite at your age | LION WITCH WARDROBE | 2/15 |
| 6. A book from the Old Testament (or a retelling of an Old Testament story) | DANIEL IN THE LION'S DEN | 9/25 |
| 7. A book from the New Testament (or a retelling of a New Testament story) | | |
| 8. A book based on a true story | HERBERT: BRAVE SEA DOG | 9/3 |
| 9. A book your pastor or Sunday School teacher recommends | | |
| 10. A book more than 100 years old | BLACK BEAUTY | |
| 11. A book about families | GONE CRAZY IN ALABAMA | 9/22 |
| 12. A book about relationships or friendship | CRAFTILY EVER AFTER | 9/8 |
| 13. A book featuring someone of a different ethnicity than you | WAGON WHEELS | 9/9 |

www.timberdoodle.com • ©2020

| The Challenge | The Book You Chose | Date Completed |
|---|---|---|
| 14. A book about someone who came from another country | ALL THE WAY TO AMERICA | 9|3 |
| 15. A book of fairy tales or folk tales (or an extended retelling of one) | JACK & THE BEANSTALK | 9|20 |
| 16. A book recommended by a parent or sibling | BABY SITTERS CLUB | 10|16 |
| 17. A book by or about a missionary | | |
| 18. A Caldecott, Newbery, or Geisel Award winner | THE TALE OF DESPERAUX | 9|27 |
| 19. A book about a holiday | FAMILY UNDER THE BRIDGE | 9|28 |
| 20. A book about grandparents or senior citizens | I AM MY GRANDPA'S ENKELIN | 10|2 |
| 21. A book with visual puzzles | I SPY BOOK | 9|25 |
| 22. A book that has a fruit in its title | HOW TO MAKE CHERRY PIE | 10|17 |
| 23. A book about a farm | BABE | 9|14 |
| 24. A book about illness or medicine | THE LEMONADE CLUB | 9|21 |
| 25. A book about learning, school, or a teacher | STEAMBOAT SCHOOL | 10|7 |
| 26. A graphic novel | HEREVILLE | 10|6 |

**THE COMMITTED READER**

| The Challenge | The Book You Chose | Date Completed |
|---|---|---|
| 27. A book of poetry | NEW KID ON THE BLOCK | 10/3 |
| 28. A book with a great cover | PRINCE CASPIAN | 2/20 |
| 29. A book about food | THE CHOCOLATE TOUCH | 10/6 |
| 30. A book about weather | | |
| 31. A book about an adventure | SOUTH POLE PIG | 12/1 |
| 32. A book by or about William Shakespeare (or a retelling of one of his plays) | WILLIAM SHAKESPEAR GRAPHIC NOVEL | 9/13 |
| 33. A funny book | PAUL BUNYAN | 10/22 |
| 34. A mystery or detective story | BOXCAR CHILDREN | 10/27 |
| 35. A picture book | GO DOG GO | 3/1 |
| 36. A book by or about a famous American | PRESIDENT STUCK IN BATHTUB | 10/19 |
| 37. A book about the Renaissance | MARGARITE MAKES A BOOK | 2/21 |
| 38. A book about early American history | A KIDS GUIDE TO NATIVE AMERICAN | 9/30 |
| 39. A book about money | TOOTHPASTE MILLIONAIRE | 12/6 |

| The Challenge | The Book You Chose | Date Completed |
|---|---|---|
| 40. A book about art or artists | FRIDA & HER ANIMALITOS | 2/20 |
| 41. A book about music or a musician | SWING SISTERS | 12/17 |
| 42. A book about an invention or inventor | BOO BOOS THAT CHANGE THE W. | 12/6 |
| 43. A book of crafts or games | SIDE WALK CHALK | 12/3 |
| 44. A book about a boy | HENRY HUGGINS | 12/11 |
| 45. A book about a girl | AMERICAN GIRL - KIRSTEN | 2/25 |
| 46. A book about books or a library | BOB THE ALIEN | 2/28 |
| 47. A book about adoption | | |
| 48. A book about someone who is differently abled (blind, deaf, mentally handicapped, etc.) | SONG FOR AWHALE | 2/17 |
| 49. A book you or your family owns but you've never read | | |
| 50. A book about babies | | |
| 51. A book about writing | | |
| 52. A book made into a movie (but read the book first!) | | |

| The Challenge | The Book You Chose | Date Completed |
|---|---|---|
| 53. A book about prayer | | |
| 54. A book recommended by a librarian or teacher | LASSIE | 2/22 |
| 55. An encyclopedia, dictionary, or almanac | FARM ANATOMY | 3/1 |
| 56. A book about building or architecture | | |
| 57. A biography of a world leader | | |
| 58. A book published the same year you (the student) were born | | |
| 59. A book with a one-word title | TODAY | 2/12 |
| 60. A book or magazine about a career you're interested in | | |
| 61. A book about siblings | RAMONA BEEZUS | 3/2 |
| 62. A book about animals | | |
| 63. A book featuring a dog | WHITE FANG | 3/5 |
| 64. A book featuring a horse | | |
| 65. A book you have started but never finished | SWISS FAMILY ROBINSON | 1/20 |
| 66. A book about plants or gardening | NATURE ANATOMY | ALL |
| 67. A book about a hobby or a skill you want to learn | | |
| 68. A book of comics | GARFIELD | 2/2 |
| 69. A book about a famous war | THE REVOLUTIONARY WAR | 10/1 |
| 70. A book about sports | | |
| 71. A book about math (numbers, mathematicians, patterns...) | | |
| 72. A book about suffering or poverty | | |
| 73. A book by your favorite author | FARM, NATURE, OCEAN ANATOMY | ALL YEAR |
| 74. A book you've read before | BLACK BEAUTY | 2/22 |
| 75. A book with an ugly cover | | |
| 76. A Christian novel | | |
| 77. A book about travel or transportation | | |
| 78. A book about the natural world | | |
| 79. A biography of an author | | |
| 80. A book published in 2020–2021 | | |

www.timberdoodle.com • ©2020

| The Challenge | The Book You Chose | Date Completed |
|---|---|---|
| 81. A historical fiction book | | |
| 82. A book about science or a scientist | | |
| 83. A book about safety or survival | | |
| 84. A book about space or an astronaut | | |
| 85. A book set in Central or South America | | |
| 86. A book set in Africa | | |
| 87. A book set in Asia | | |
| 88. A book set in Europe | | |
| 89. A book with a color in its title | | |
| 90. A book about manners | | |
| 91. A book about spring | | |
| 92. A book about summer | | |
| 93. A book about autumn | | |
| 94. A book about winter | | |
| 95. A book from the 000–099 section in the Dewey Decimal shelves of your library | | |
| 96. A book from the 100–199 section in the Dewey Decimal shelves of your library | | |
| 97. A book from the 200–299 section in the Dewey Decimal shelves of your library | | |
| 98. A book from the 300–399 section in the Dewey Decimal shelves of your library | | |
| 99. A book from the 400–499 section in the Dewey Decimal shelves of your library | | |
| 100. A book from the 500–599 section in the Dewey Decimal shelves of your library | | |
| 101. A book from the 600–699 section in the Dewey Decimal shelves of your library | | |
| 102. A book from the 700–799 section in the Dewey Decimal shelves of your library | | |
| 103. A book from the 800–899 section in the Dewey Decimal shelves of your library | | |
| 104. A book from the 900–999 section in the Dewey Decimal shelves of your library | | |

## PRACTICE MAKES PERFECT

Reading is probably the most important skill your child will practice this year. Whether he is a natural reader or one who doesn't enjoy reading, it is critical to make reading as fun and rewarding as possible now.

Our experience is that the best way to cultivate an eager reader is to constantly supply him with reading materials that interest him. Future doctors may want to read up on anatomy, young explorers are drawn to the escapades of adventurers young and old, and the baby-lover in your family will be captivated by adoption stories.

Knowing how hard it can be to load the whole family up and get to the library, we're also including a brilliant anthology of reading material in your Mosdos book this year. With so many excellent selections, every student is sure to find some that resonate deeply with him and others that he would never have chosen for himself but that he finds surprisingly interesting. Assign reading as needed, but encourage it at all costs; a child who enjoys reading will find it easier to excel in every area.

# OH YAY! WRITING!

## LET'S WRITE PURPOSEFULLY

Take a good look at your child's abilities and writing readiness before insisting that he complete all of the written portions, particularly of Mosdos. Here are the writing assignments you can anticipate this year:

### Spelling You See
The motor movements of physically writing will help him retain the spelling he's learning here. It's designed to be used for only 10 minutes a day so it shouldn't be overwhelming.

### Daily 6-Trait Writing
Each lesson is wonderfully short, and this course doesn't even begin until the 12th week of school. Winner!

### First Language Lessons
I think this is the book that will be most intimidating out of the box simply because of its sheer size. Take a breath, though, and really look at it. You'll find generous white space and lessons that truly won't take that long to do. This is the one place your child will be learning grammar this year, so yes, it's important.

### Mosdos
We love this for its literature–isn't it beautiful? However, you're already covering writing, so we highly recommend skipping the writing activities in the student reader. The student workbook (and possibly the oral review questions) is great for reading comprehension, so do that — just skip the writing or allow oral answers.

### CursiveLogic
We'd encourage you to consider prioritizing this even if your child is a reluctant writer. Learning cursive has some real benefits that may help make the rest of his writing easier (see page 42).

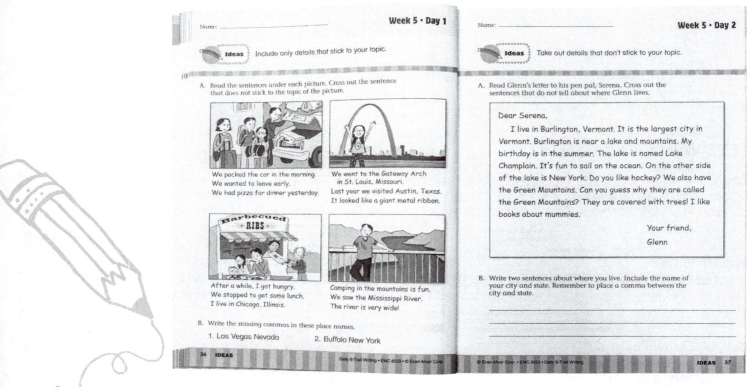

# 6-TRAIT WRITING

## BASIC ~ COMPLETE ~ ELITE

Are you familiar with trait writing? Trait-based writing is an impressive method educators have developed to determine whether a child's writing is skilled or not.

The six traits or characteristics that shape quality writing are content; organization; word choice; sentence fluency; voice; and conventions, which include grammar, spelling, and mechanics. It may sound ominous, but Daily 6-Trait Writing has made it effortless.

These short daily assignments are designed to build skills

without being overwhelming. We love them for their brevity, but also because they are so thorough!

### Scheduling

Designed for one short lesson a day, ending after 25 weeks of school. Most will likely wish to begin this on the 12th week of school and finish it with the rest of the materials, which will let you ease into the year. If you prefer, you could opt to only do three to four days' work each week so that you don't finish too early.

# SPELLING YOU SEE

## BASIC ~ COMPLETE ~ ELITE

This multisensory spelling program will help your child become a confident, successful speller, naturally and at his own speed. Because Spelling You See encourages visual memory rather than rote memory, there are no weekly spelling lists or tests and very little instructor preparation. Each daily lesson in Spelling You See: Americana uses real words presented in context within nonfiction stories about American history and culture.

Spelling You See: Americana is colorful, short, to the point, and fun!

### Scheduling

The 36 weeks of work, with five daily activities each week, are already planned out for you. Just open and go!

### ONE NOTE:

Ideally you will not complete more than one short spelling lesson every day for best retention. If your student is at all intimidated by the lesson length, keep in mind that there is enough work in each lesson to teach a speedy writer, but a more methodical writer could be overwhelmed trying to complete it all. Consider starting a timer for 10 to 15 minutes when you begin the day's work and stop where you are when it rings. The next day, just move on to the new lesson.

Also, if you do a four-day week, you only do the first four days' work and skip the fifth. It seems unusual to all of us who feel one must finish every page, but this course is designed to be most effective when used that way.

# MOSDOS LITERATURE
## BASIC ~ COMPLETE ~ ELITE

Mosdos Literature is a complete literature program that cheerily reinforces the universal ideals of courage, honesty, loyalty, and compassion. We found this such a breath of fresh air in comparison to more "sensational" readers that glamorize evil or present subject matter that is not age-appropriate.

Mosdos Literature begins with the student readers which are beautifully illustrated using a generous amount of

full-color photographs, color drawings, and black-and-white pictures. Your student will complete the Sunflower Reader first, then move on to the Daisy Reader.

Before each story in the student reader, there is an introduction to the story and an explanation of some facet of literature. That literary focus can include character, theme, internal and external conflicts, setting, climax, foreshadowing, and more. This literary component is developed and illuminated through the stories. Vocabulary words that might be unfamiliar are presented in boxes on the pages where the words first appear in the account.

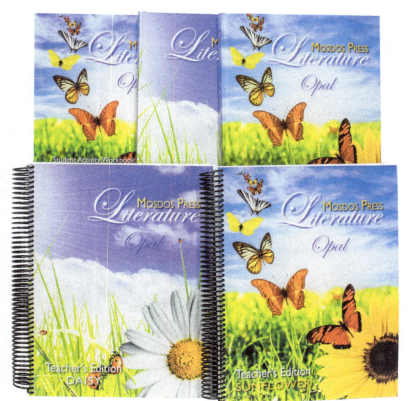

The stories are followed not just by the classic review questions designed to assess reading comprehension, but also by more complex questions that require thoughtful analysis. Every unit concludes with activities such as writing a short skit, doing a craft, or memorizing a poem. Pick the ones that best suit your child; there are far too many to do them all. Unless your child is a budding author, you can minimize the writing activities. Your child is already doing a lot of writing this year in Daily 6-Trait Writing and First Language Lessons.

Next is the consumable, colorful, and engaging student activity workbook. For nearly every story in the student reader, the workbook contains corresponding vocabulary, creative writing, or comprehension questions, while also providing extended reinforcement of the literary elements

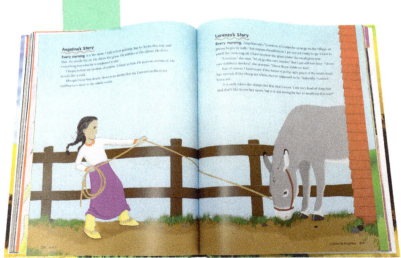

being taught. These assignments help you to evaluate areas of progress or concepts that might require additional work.

The advantage of Mosdos Press is that the literature, vocabulary, and application components tie together, giving your child a chance to truly understand what was taught by approaching it in a variety of ways.

Through great commentary plus questions and answers, the Teacher's Edition will make lively discussions with your child possible. Each page of the student reader is duplicated at a smaller size in the Teacher's Edition, yet it is still abundantly easy to read. Information is arranged in the ample margins around these replicated pages, discussing the literary components found in each story with clear, concise explanations. Of course, the Teacher's Guide also includes the answers for the student activity workbook.

## Scheduling
Don't worry! This is easier to use than it appears at first glance.

You have six units in the course, all helpfully labeled in the

Teacher's Edition. A typical unit is further broken down into five subsections, and there is a helpful week-by-week sample schedule on pages 96-99 in this handbook.

If you're more of a grab-and-go person, you may find it easiest to remember that a week's work will typically begin with the Lesson in Literature and include reading until you reach the next Lesson in Literature.

Our family would have chosen to answer the Studying the Selection questions in the readers orally. If time allowed, we might have selected one Focus or Creating and Writing activity to complete for further study. In most cases, however, we suggest skipping the writing since you'll be covering that with Daily 6-Trait Writing.

Note that the last unit in the book, "A Toad for Tuesday," looks a bit different visually and comprises three weeks' work.

Busy families may choose to skip the Unit Wrap-ups, while others who enjoy the hands-on activities can complete them.

This course naturally breaks into 30 units. If you have a traditional 36-week school year you have several fantastic options:

1. Take a week off after each unit
2. Move the Unit Wrap-ups to a week of their own.
3. Would you perhaps prefer to finish early?
4. Or, use the six extra weeks as free passes for particularly hectic weeks.

You decide!

# CURSIVELOGIC

## BASIC ~ COMPLETE ~ ELITE

Research now reports a clear connection between handwriting and language, as well as between memory and critical thinking skills. A student who takes notes by hand performs better than students who take notes on laptops, both in understanding and recall. Moreover, writing letters (especially in cursive) as opposed to viewing them on a screen is associated with more advanced brain function.

If you have a child who struggles with learning cursive then CursiveLogic may be just what you need. Using a multi-sensory approach with four basic shapes, CursiveLogic will teach your child proper formation and connection for all letters in just 10 weeks.

Rather than teaching each letter individually, CursiveLogic teaches all the letters that share a common shape at once. Each group of letters is color-coded to help your student readily recall the initial strokes as he learns them; bright orange, lime green, silver, and mauve capture students' attention. Using colored pencils and pens can add even more to the learning and the fun.

However, when your child has advanced to tracing and writing words that combine letters from different groups, he should not stop and switch writing instruments in the middle of a word to match the color coding. It is more important that he learn to write continuously at that stage, so he'll need to use just one color.

CursiveLogic includes information about grip, body and hand placement, suggestions for left-handed students, and more.

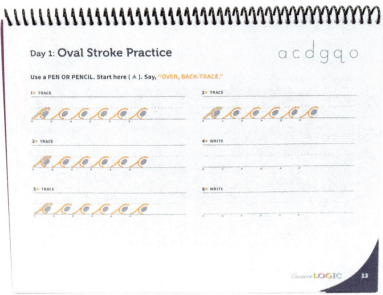

### Scheduling

This book is designed as a 10-week course, and we think you'll see maximum impact by using it as designed. We'd suggest starting your year with this one as your child will then be able to use his new skills for the rest of his school year. Plus, you'll finish CursiveLogic just a week before beginning Daily 6-Trait Writing, which makes it easy on your schedule.

You'll quickly notice that each week includes three to four "days" of work, with multiple pages per day. This is intentional, and it is paced to build maximum skills. You'll just want to flex the rest of your student's work load around it.

Also, you'll find 14 practice pages to complete after finishing the course. We suggest one a week to keep your student's skills sharp.

# FIRST LANGUAGE LESSONS

BASIC ~ **COMPLETE ~ ELITE**

This is the backbone of your child's grammar this year, and (happy dance) First Language Lessons requires very little teacher prep; just open the instruction manual, read the script, and follow directions to teach the concepts.

The student workbook has appealing fonts and plenty of white space, so the individual pages are less intimidating for children. Do not be alarmed by the size of these books!

Each lesson is designed to take 30 minutes or less. In fact, the author suggests that if your student's lesson time exceeds 30 minutes, stop for the day, then continue with the remainder of the lesson the following day. Also, if a student is struggling to understand or if he doesn't write easily, he may do some of the written exercises orally instead.

By the time you've finished the course, you will have covered a full range of grammar topics, including parts of speech, punctuation, sentence diagrams, and skills in beginning writing and storytelling.

Does that seem like a lot for third grade? The premise of First Language Lessons is that students are almost always ready for more, if we will just take the time to teach them.

First Language Lessons' spiral learning method ensures mastery for every child, important for these foundational years of language study.

## Scheduling

Do two to three lessons per week. If you choose to do the optional end lessons about writing letters, oral lessons, and dictionary skills, then plan on doing three lessons every week.

# BEGINNING WORD ROOTS

~~BASIC~~ ~~COMPLETE~~ **ELITE**

Children who have a solid grasp of word roots are bound to be children with better reading comprehension skills, primarily because they have acquired the ability to decode words.

It may not surprise you, then, to hear that according to national standards, students in grades 4 to 12 must now be able to demonstrate their knowledge of how to use common Greek and Latin roots for analyzing the meaning of complex words.

Learning word elements also dramatically improves spelling and the ability to decode unfamiliar words. Word Roots will add hundreds of words to your child's vocabulary and greater depth to his thinking and writing.

Your child will be getting a jump start this year with Beginning Word Roots. It will teach your child the meanings of Latin prefixes, roots, and suffixes of words commonly used in English without much effort. Just grab the workbook and go!

## Scheduling

With 24 lessons plus 3 review chapters, we suggest completing 1 lesson or review chapter a week. This will either let you finish nine weeks early or allow you to defer or split a lesson up to nine times. However, if you prefer to work by page count, just do about three pages a week.

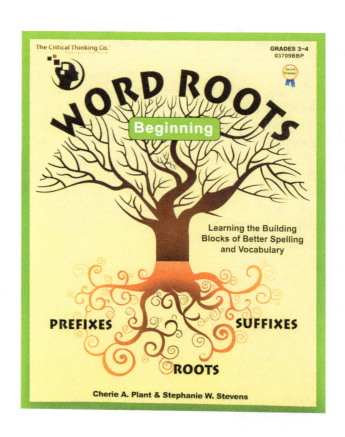

# THE ADVENTURES OF ROBIN HOOD

Many families have found that graphic novels provide huge incentives to their budding readers. We've included the story of Robin Hood for this year. If your child loves it, you'll know where to start at your local library, and even if he doesn't love it, he will have been exposed to famous literature.

## Scheduling

We suggest not assigning this book, but just letting him read it and see what he thinks. You could even use it for book #26 in the Reading Challenge!

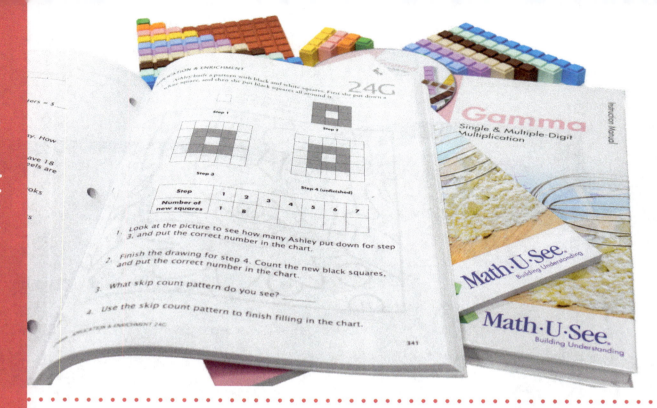

## HANDS-ON MATH

Basic math is a critical skill for your child to master, whether he grows up to be a carpenter, doctor, accountant, or farmer. But all too often math programs rely on memorization instead of comprehension, leaving the student at a disadvantage.

That's not going to happen to your child! The real-world math problems posed in Math-U-See (combined with the hands-on manipulatives) create an unbeatable math program.

With simple, uncluttered pages, Math-U-See is mastery-oriented, clear, to the point, and effective. In Math-U-See, new ideas are introduced step by step in a logical order, while concepts that have been mastered are reviewed periodically.

Math-U-See's teacher guide and supplemental DVD will teach more than just how to solve a math problem. They will also show why the problem is solved in this manner and when to apply the concept. On the DVDs, each lesson is demonstrated with kind-hearted enthusiasm. DVDs can be played on a DVD player or computer; however, Windows 10 users will need to download a separate video player.

While Math-U-See still requires a fair amount of parental involvement, by this grade your child will be able to work more independently. The instruction manual can be read by your child and, of course, he will want to watch the DVD presentation before beginning each lesson. The instruction manuals also include complete answers with step-by-step solutions for all the exercises and tests, and there is extra instruction for the enrichment problems.

Math-U-See is laid out with step-by-step procedures for introducing, practicing, mastering, and reviewing concepts. How do you know when your child has "mastered" a math concept? Not just when he gets the answers right, but when he can teach the concept back, especially if he is able to do so with a word problem. Math-U-See will show you how.

You will want to decide as you start the year whether your student will be completing the optional "Application and Enrichment" section of each lesson—sometimes considered the honors portion. If these challenges overwhelm your student, you should skip them or offer generous assistance. Otherwise, embrace them for the opportunity they are to help him learn more skills and train his brain to think logically.

It's worth mentioning that there are other reasons your child may not need to complete every one of these pages. At the risk of oversimplifying, the practice worksheets (A, B, C) are to be used with the manipulatives until your child reaches an "aha!" moment and grasps the lesson. He may then move to the review pages (D, E, F) and should at least complete worksheet D in its entirety. If he's

breezing through the pages, you have several great options. He could complete every other problem, or he could skip E or F or both. (You do want to be sure he's not rusty on any of those problems before skipping, though—many students will do best completing all or most of the D, E, F worksheets.) Worksheet G is the application/enrichment/extra-credit page. It's okay to skip but valuable to complete.

### Scheduling
You have 30 lessons to complete, so we suggest planning on 1 lesson a week, including the DVD as well as the textbook/workbook portions and any relevant tests. However, as Mr. Demme points out, some lessons will take you longer than others to achieve mastery. If you find yourself "stuck" on a lesson, feel free to allow it to take you an extra week. Just don't do that more than six times this year!

# MÖBI MAX
## ~~BASIC~~ COMPLETE ~ ELITE

Multiply your child's math calculation speed while adding fun to his day with Möbi Max. This fast-paced number tile game transforms necessary math drill from tedious to exciting. Möbi's crossword-style game is made up of sturdy aqua blue number tiles and white double-sided operations tiles. Use them to make simple math equations of addition, subtraction, multiplication, and division. But make them fast, because the first player to use all of his blue tiles and yell "Möbi" wins.

Begin by separating the colors into two piles with the number tiles face down. Draw seven number tiles. Operations tiles are taken as needed, and you can use either side of the tile. Then, as fast as possible, create a "pod" of math equations to use up your number tiles. As you play, you will be adding more number tiles to your pile until all tiles from the pool are gone. To integrate newly drawn tiles you will often need to rearrange existing tiles, so your pod is always shifting. The first player who completes his pod wins.

There are many ways to play Möbi, but here are a few of our favorite variations:

### Add & Subtract
Use only the addition and subtraction tiles for the entire game.

### Chill Möbi
Divide all the number tiles evenly among the players at the start of the game.

### Number of the Day
Pick a number, then every player must include that number somewhere in each of his equations.

### My Number Is _
Every player has his own "number of the day" and must use it in every equation.

### On My Pod
Every player is given a sum for one of his problems (make every player's the same or use bigger numbers for those who need more of a challenge). Each player must keep that sum in his pod at all times.

### Mandatory Multiplication
If your student is ready for more of a challenge, or if you really want to work on multiplication skills, require him to use at least one multiplication (or division) tile in every equation.

### Scheduling
This game is truly unlimited. We suggest breaking it out once a week and playing a game or two to keep your child's skills sharp.

# WRAP-UPS MULTIPLICATION

Even though math should never be just a drill, it is a rare child who would not benefit from some drill work. Wrap-ups are convenient, portable, self-contained, and, best of all, self-correcting!

### Scheduling
Start using these Wrap-ups after your child has learned the concept of multiplication. We suggest getting this set out at least once a week until he has mastered it.

# EXTREME DOT-TO-DOT

Kick-start your student's mental focus with the amazing Extreme Dot-to-Dot: Baby Animals. Unlike conventional dot-to-dot puzzles that reveal too much of the picture and ruin the mystery, Extreme Dot-to-Dot: Baby Animals' puzzles are intricate and so challenging that when your student looks at a page, he will have no idea what the end result will be.

Mapping and concentration are just two of the educational benefits to solving these dot-to-dot puzzles. Both your student's left brain and right brain will be exercised as he works to complete puzzles containing 510 to over 1,600 dots. Some puzzles even cover a two-page spread — definitely not for the faint-hearted.

### Scheduling
With 32 puzzles in all, completing 1 a week will set a perfect pace.

## THIS IS AS CRITICAL AS IT IS APPEALING

In Timberdoodle's curriculum kits, you will find a rigorous pursuit of thinking skills for every child, in every grade. This is simply not an optional skill for your child. A child who can think logically will be able to learn well and teach himself logically in ways that an untrained brain will find difficult.

Be thankful that you won't have to persuade your child to learn to think, though – he's wired for problem solving! We're guessing this portion of the curriculum will be the hardest not to race through. After all, who doesn't want to work through a creative thinking skills puzzle book, solve the mystery of wiring the circuit, or beat you in a quick round of Anomia Kids?

# CRITICAL & CREATIVE

## BASIC ~ COMPLETE ~ ELITE

It is nearly impossible to overemphasize thinking skills when planning a child's education. A student who doesn't know how to think things through will be at a disadvantage in every area of study.

This course specifically features the relationship between critical and creative thought. While often misunderstood, profound thinking requires both imagination and intellectual ideas. To produce excellence in thinking, we need to engage our children in a curriculum that overlaps the logical and the imaginative sides of thinking.

Critical & Creative's 46 theme-based units will give your child lots of practice thinking in a variety of ways. From brainteasers and logic puzzles to mazes, Venn diagrams, and secret codes, Critical & Creative Thinking Activities has a wealth of mind-boggling activities that your child will enjoy while he learns thinking fluency, originality, generalizing, patterning, and problem solving.

### Scheduling
While you could split this by pages (four a week), we suggest instead completing one to two units a week so that you don't lose the continuity and fun of doing all the pages on a certain topic at once.

**Note:** While we find Critical & Creative to be a very valuable series, it is published by a secular publisher, and our conservative family would at least have skipped pages 8-10.

# CIRCUIT MAZE

~~BASIC~~ **COMPLETE ~ ELITE**

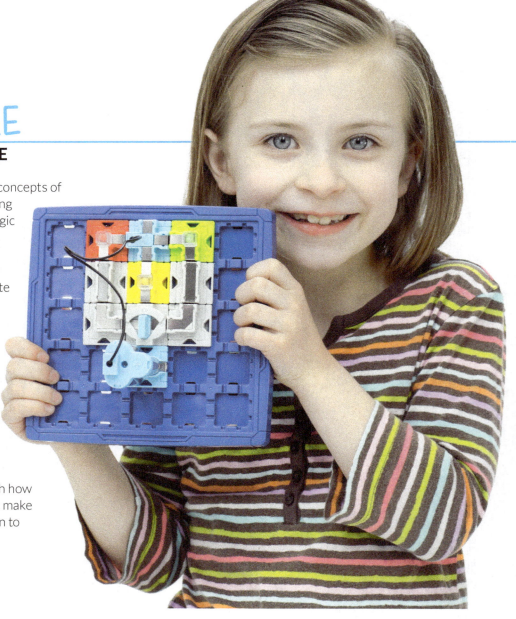

Circuit Maze safely teaches complex concepts of electricity in a creative and entertaining way with a series of circuit-building logic puzzles.

Select one of 60 cards, then place the shown pieces on the board to complete the circuit and light up the beacons.

Circuit Maze puts the principles and concepts of electrical circuits right into your child's hands. Simple and advanced circuitry concepts are explored, such as series circuits, parallel circuits, series and parallel circuits in combination, and parallel circuits in bypass.

Reasoning and logic skills coupled with how electricity and electrical circuits work make Circuit Maze a wonderful introduction to electrical engineering.

## Scheduling
Solve one to two puzzles each week.

# ANOMIA KIDS

Anomia Kids is a loud, hilarious, high-energy game that both kids and adults will enjoy playing. Playfully illustrated and easy to learn, Anomia Kids will have your whole family sharpening their thinking, visual perception, and speech-language skills.

The directions are simple. Draw a card from the center pile, flip it over, and see if the symbol matches another player's card. If it does, you must quickly blurt out a word that begins with the same sound as the illustration before your opponent does the same. Whoever shouts first (because let's be honest, this is not a game for inside voices) wins that round.

The creator of Anomia Kids knows that even though our minds are full of all kinds of information, when under pressure our brains have trouble with word and sound association and recall. Anomia Kids will broaden language skills as players strive to remember multiple words that can work for a given picture. It can even be used to strengthen foreign language skills, so it would be a perfect drill for a foreign language co-op of which your child is a part. Anomia Kids is a National Parent Product Awards winner for 2018.

## Scheduling

Unlimited. We suggest pulling it out once a week and playing a few games. Beginning readers and up may play, so involve as much of the family as is available for whole family learning and fun!

## HOW DID SAMURAI BECOME SUMO WRESTLERS?

Many history curriculum options make the mistake of focusing solely on U.S.A. history. As important as that is, doesn't it make more sense to start with the big picture of history? This year you'll learn about the Early Modern Times, covering the major historical events in the years 1600 – 1850, from Elizabeth I to the Forty-Niners. You'll answer questions like:

Who was the Sun King?
What was the Black Hole of Calcutta?
Why was a California town named Ground Hog Glory?
And, of course, how did samurai become sumo wrestlers?

Geography this year will be equally intriguing as you build your own Puzzleball globe. Additionally, complete the vibrant pages of Skill Sharpeners Geography to master important geography concepts.

With True Stories of the Revolutionary War, you will also get to learn more about early American history through the true accounts of the people who lived through it.

# STORY OF THE WORLD

This is very easy to use. Just have your child read one section from the story book, then ask him to tell you what it was about. Afterwards, pick an activity page or worksheet that is appropriate for your child's interest and your schedule.

Did you see how big the activity book is? Keep in mind that one of the activity book's biggest advantages is the fact that it offers a wide range of activities for each lesson. Pick the ones that best fit your child's learning style and your family's schedule, but don't try to do them all!

One brilliant way to use this text is to approach it from a notebooking perspective. To do this, you'll want to grab your child a blank notebook that he will fill with his recap ("narration") of each chapter. As he goes he'll add art, maps, and even photos of more tangible projects that he does. This is a somewhat labor intensive approach, but if you're eager for your child to have a firm grasp on world history it will be hard to beat that method for helping him retain what he learns.

### Scheduling

Completing three chapters every two weeks is a realistic pace that will get you through the books in just under a year.

If you purchased the Elite kit, you'll love having the audio book. It includes the same content as the story

book, but it can be much more convenient. Your child can just pop in the CD and listen to his history with as many of the family as would like to participate. What a treat!

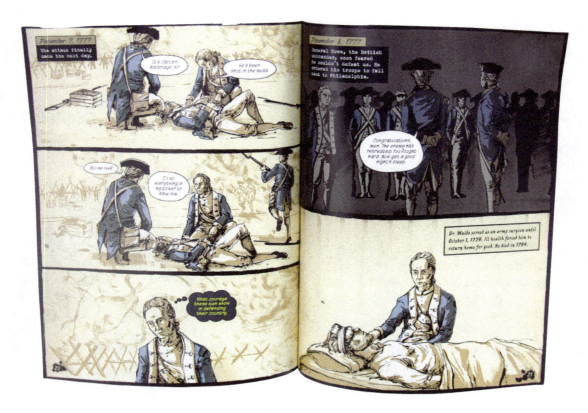

# TRUE STORIES OF THE REVOLUTIONARY WAR

~~BASIC~~ **COMPLETE ~ ELITE**

Many families have found that graphic novels provide huge incentives to their budding readers. The pictures will help your student to stay focused and make him want to understand the written text.

You'll be thrilled that he's not only enjoying reading, but also getting a memorable, insightful look at history. Be forewarned, though, that war is far from pretty. However, this series does a tasteful job of showing what it would have been like to live through these events without depicting unnecessary gore.

Learn more about the Revolutionary War through the accounts of the people who lived through it. Experience the terror of a sneak attack and read how a mother risked her life by spying for the colonists. True Stories of the Revolutionary War gives a quick glimpse of well-known battles that shaped our nation.

### Scheduling
We suggest not assigning this book, but just letting your student read it and see what he thinks. Or save it for when it ties into The Story of the World in chapter 22.

# SKILL SHARPENERS GEOGRAPHY

~~BASIC~~ **COMPLETE ~ ELITE**

Skill Sharpeners Geography lets your child explore his world while learning key map skills and geography concepts with little fuss on your part. The cross-curricular activities integrate the most current geography standards, and each eye-catching book is divided into colorful collections of engaging, grade-appropriate themes.

Each theme includes short nonfiction reading selections, comprehension questions, vocabulary practice, and writing prompts.

In this grade, each chapter has a rhythm to it. First there are a couple of pages of reading, a few questions, and some visual literacy exercises—usually maps or the like. Next is a page of vocabulary practice, using fun things such as crosswords or wordsearches, etc. Then, you'll find an involved hands-on activity such as designing a passport or performing an archaeological dig. (This is an optional project; consider it extra credit!) Finally, you'll find a writing exercise. While the prompts are worthy, not every student needs this extra writing practice. If it's too much for your child, we suggest having him simply answer verbally or record his answers on your phone.

Skill Sharpeners Geography takes your child beyond just the basics of geography and includes a smattering of histories and cultures within our world. The colorful illustrations and pages will grab your child's attention, and the handy (removable) answer key in the back allows you to help your student easily check his work.

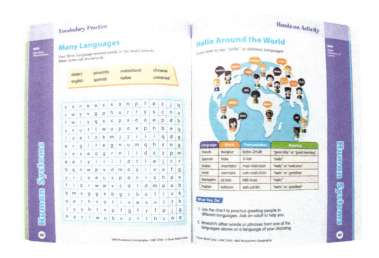

## Scheduling

With 132 pages in all this year, simply complete 4 a week to stay on track. Add in the activities as time and interest allow.

And yes, you may truly skip the activity and writing pages (with no guilt) if that isn't how your child learns best.

# FAMOUS FIGURES
~~BASIC~~ ~~COMPLETE~~ **ELITE**

With Famous Figures of the Early Modern Era, you'll find that history becomes hands-on as you assemble movable figures of 21 of the historical figures of the early modern era, such as Queen Nzinga, Peter the Great, and Robert Fulton.

While listening to The Story of the World, your avid artist can color in the detailed figures. Using mini brads and a 1/8" hole punch for assembly will allow their arms and legs to move into whatever pose is needed.

For the meticulous child who wants it colored exactly right, matching pre-colored action figures are also included.

Don't forget about the detailed biography section in 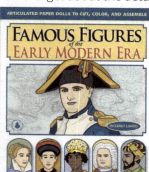 the front of the book which provides key information about the characters. A companion reading list for each figure is also included, which is perfect if your child wants to learn more or if you're looking for a relevant book for him to read this week.

## Scheduling

We suggest completing these figures when you encounter each in Story of the World. Across the page you'll see the chapters each is mentioned in, or for the few not directly covered in Story of the World, you'll see our idea of where to slide them in to stay with the timeframe/topic of the chapter.

Are you looking for ways to use the completed figures?

- Your child could put on a puppet show re-enacting a historic moment or imagining a more ordinary part of their day. (For added fun, make a video of the performance.)

- Use one or more of the figures to create a diorama or display representing either the timeframe or a particular event.

- Do you use a timeline? Add these figures to it!

- And, of course, allow your child to engage in creative play with the figures. Sometimes they will capture the imagination in a way that no written text alone will.

**Where to Insert the Figures into Story of the World:**

Mary, Queen of Scots–chapter 2

*Rembrandt–chapter 2

James I of England–chapter 3

Pocahontas–chapter 3

Samuel de Champlain–chapter 4

Queen Nzinga–chapter 7

Shah Jahan–chapter 11

Louis XIV–chapter 13

*Johann Sebastian Bach–chapter 14

William Penn–chapter 15

Isaac Newton–chapter 16

Peter the Great–chapter 17

Ch'ien-lung–chapter 20

Captain James Cook–chapter 24

Catherine the Great–chapter 26

*Robert Fulton–chapter 27

Napoleon Bonaparte–chapters 29 and 33

Sacagawea–chapter 32

William Clark–chapter 32

Simón Bolívar–chapter 34

William Wilberforce–chapter 36

*Not specifically mentioned in Story of the World 3, but pertinent to the named chapter/timeframe

# PUZZLEBALL GLOBE

~~BASIC~~ ~~COMPLETE~~ **ELITE**

Puzzles can be educational in so many ways because they stretch your child's brain and improve the way his mind solves problems. While he's solving a puzzle, he's really teaching his brain to work in new ways. As your child solves a geography puzzle, he is mentally drilling himself with physical facts, such as what country goes next to the one he has just completed. Subconsciously, he is making a number of associations as he searches for the next piece.

Flat puzzles of spherical items are easier to assemble, but what if you could hone your geographical skills on something more appropriate, more true-to-life? Now you can, with the Puzzleball Globe. The Puzzleball Globe can be assembled in three different ways. First, use the small number located on each of the curved, non-image sides of the puzzle piece for easy, systematic assembly. For more of a challenge, use a world map to assemble the globe. Finally, when you think you are ready for the expert level, try assembling the Puzzleball Globe looking only at the puzzle–not your map, the box, or the numbers behind each piece.

Decked with animals and landmarks, the Puzzleball Globe consists of 180 beautiful, vibrantly colored, curved, and perfectly crafted puzzle pieces that allow for an exact fit. It is easily assembled with no glue required! A stand is included to display your work of art, but you will have so much fun putting the globe together over and over that you shouldn't be surprised if the stand gets little use!

## Scheduling
We suggest having your child complete this once a month until it is too easy for him.

## READY TO EXPERIMENT?

With Science in the Scientific Revolution, your student will discover what a bishop's hat has to do with the heart's mitral valve, flip a coin before reading Pascal's wager, count candies to learn about population estimates, and accelerate a wagon of books to experience the importance of seat belts.

The third book in the Berean Science series, Science in the Scientific Revolution covers scientific developments from 1543 to the end of the 1600s. Students will see that most of the great natural philosophers of this time were Christians who studied the world to learn more about the God who created it.

Your student is also going to love the Dr. Bonyfide series! He'll study the bones of his hands, arms, and shoulders while having a blast with this captivating, colorful book.

# SCIENCE IN THE SCIENTIFIC REVOLUTION

~~BASIC~~ **COMPLETE ~ ELITE**

Berean Science offers students an opportunity to study science through the lens of history. Using a narrative dialogue and a Christian worldview, Berean Science teaches science chronologically, so there are vast and varied science topics in each volume.

Fairly bursting with experiments–every lesson has some sort of activity–Berean Science's strong focus on this hands-on component makes it an ideal program for the wigglers in your household.

The durable hardcover textbook has lots of full-color illustrations. The lessons are concise but complete, drilling down to the core of what your child needs to know. Lesson material is often just a page or two following each activity, perfect for any child who struggles to sit and pay attention.

The activities, all color-coded and easy to find quickly, often involve inexpensive household items and are the gateway to the exploration of each scientific concept. Plus, each book has a helpful section in the front that tells you all the materials you will need, broken down per chapter, for doing the experiments.

Each lesson concludes with questions or additional activities for "younger," "older," and "oldest" students, so Berean Science lends itself well to multi-grade homes that prefer to use just one science curriculum for the entire family.

Lessons are taught directly from the text, so there is no

cumbersome teacher's manual.

If your student appreciates beginning with notebooking pages to reduce his writing, you'll appreciate the notebook included in your Elite kit. (Didn't choose an Elite kit this year? Check out the free PDFs from the publisher on our website.)

## Scheduling

You'll notice that some of the lessons in your book are red in the index. A red lesson indicates that this lesson is optional–a bonus lesson, if you will.

If you wish to only complete essential lessons, just do two lessons a week. However, if you prefer to enjoy every single lesson, you'll want to do two to three lessons a week. (In fact, if you alternate between two and three lessons, you'll come out exactly on track.)

## Pro Tip:

The most intimidating part of science can be gathering the supplies required for experiments. If you purchased the Elite kit, take advantage of the lab kit included. If not, we recommend you stop now, grab a box and the list of materials printed in the introductory pages of your textbook, and collect all your needed materials,

purchasing any items you need for the year on your next shopping trip. Make it more fun by considering it a full-family scavenger hunt!

Besides everyday dishware and perishable items, you should be able to collect most other items you need, and you'll never regret having already completed the most labor-intensive step of your child's science education this year.

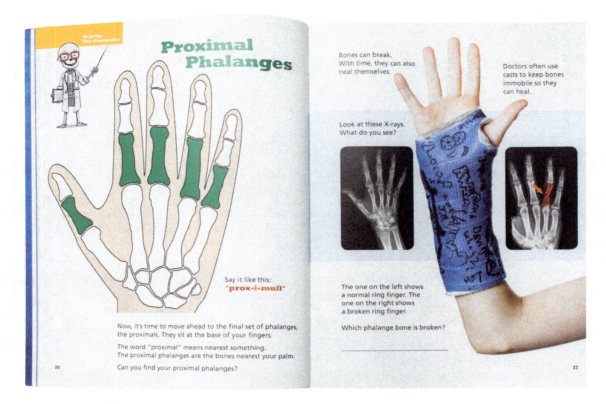

# DR. BONYFIDE 1

~~BASIC~~ **COMPLETE ~ ELITE**

Dr. Bonyfide is a young person's highly entertaining guide to his own body. You know that if your child has basic information about his body he is more likely to make healthy life choices. Plus, isn't it natural to want to understand why your body works the way it does?

Developed by a team of educators, health professionals, and parents, Dr. Bonyfide Presents will creatively guide your child through the bone structures of his body using kid-friendly jokes, rhymes, puzzles, fun facts, and original comic strips. Plus, a pair of X-ray vision (colored) glasses will let your child investigate the bones on special pages. Write-in quizzes and a range of hands-on activities will help you as a teaching parent to assess his progress while simultaneously helping him retain his new knowledge.

### Scheduling
With 108 pages in all, plan on doing 3 a week if you want to make this course last your entire school year. But be prepared—your child may find it so engaging that he races through and finishes it early!

## STEM IS EVERYWHERE!

STEM learning is more than robotics and computer programming. STEM tools include those that engage students in exploratory learning, discovery, and problem-solving; they also teach the foundational skills of critical thinking and short- and long-term planning. So STEM includes your Doodle Adventure book as well as your Circuit Maze logic game, even though they are listed in other places in this handbook. Basically anything that goes beyond a rote read-and-regurgitate lesson undoubtedly falls into the STEM classification. In assembling this guide, many of our products could easily have been classified as STEM, but these three tools seem especially appropriate for this category.

# TYPING INSTRUCTOR FOR KIDS
~~BASIC~~ **COMPLETE ~ ELITE**

Using proven typing techniques, children will master the keyboard while journeying with Toby and Lafitte to five imaginary lands where they learn proper typing techniques and build keyboarding skills. Just choose a typing plan, set a words-per-minute goal, and, as your child explores Typer Island, he will learn typing along the way.

The engaging lessons and exercises teach children important typing skills, including speed and accuracy. If your child finds your old typing program boring, and if you are looking for the right balance of education, entertainment, and motivation in a typing program, then you will appreciate Typing Instructor for Kids.

Typing Instructor for Kids offers 30-plus action-packed, multi-level game challenges; graduated drills and lesson plans; hundreds of activities, exercises, and tests; and bilingual learning in English and Spanish.

### Scheduling
The only limit is your schedule, but we suggest three lessons a week.

# GRAVITRAX DELUXE

With GraviTrax your child can design and build high-tech marble runs while using gravity, magnetism, kinetic energy, momentum, velocity, and problem solving to propel marbles to the finish.

With this open-ended construction set, your child will have access to two manuals. In the first, he will be asked to build a marble run precisely as pictured. In the second, he will be told the exact pieces and a few placements, but he will need to complete the design. We suggest starting with the "precisely as pictured" manual and then move to ones he needs to solve. Finally, mix in the Zipline add-on for divergent construction challenges.

With over 100 pieces and more than 18 different construction elements, your child will learn how physics impacts the track and his marble, and he will experiment with how height, curves, freefall, and even a magnetic cannon can control the speed of the marble. Everything a STEM building set should be, GraviTrax Deluxe combines physics, architecture, and engineering and will sharpen your child's spatial reasoning, logical planning, and architectural design skills.

### Scheduling
With 33 models to build, plus as many as your child improvises, we suggest 1 per week starting with the exact replication manual.

# SCRATCH CODING CARDS

~~BASIC~~ ~~COMPLETE~~ **ELITE**

Whenever I previewed a Scratch coding book my eyes would blur, and my mind would be planning dinner. Not so with Scratch Coding Cards; this is primarily because tasks are presented in bite-size portions.

The front of each card shows an activity, for example, animating a character or adding your voice. The back of the card shows the Scratch blocks used and how to put them together.

With the Scratch Coding Cards, your child will create interactive games, stories, music, and animations. This is a fun, motivating way to learn sequencing, conditionals, variables, and other coding concepts.

There are 10 sets of cards included, and each set includes an overview card that shows what you will be doing. It lets you know if the component cards need to be completed in a specific order or if they may be done at random.

If your family is new to Scratch coding, you will be pleased to know that an introductory booklet shows the basics of using this drag-and-drop language and how to get set up for the first time. You will need to either work online or download the offline version of Scratch–see the booklet for details.

## Scheduling

These cards offer unlimited implementations. One option would be to simply introduce two new cards each week for your child to use in a project of his liking.

Another would be to have him add a new set of cards (e.g. Animate Your Name or Let's Dance) every week for 10 weeks. Then he will have all the skills he needs to create his own projects for the rest of the year. We'd still ask him to complete an entire project of his choice each week, as simple or elaborate as his schedule allows. Get ready to watch his skills explode!

Is he at a loss on how to use his skills during weeks 11-36? Have him illustrate something from his other studies this week, tell a joke on screen, create a game for his younger sibling, or retell a favorite book or story in this simpler format.

## STEM OR STEAM?

STEM, an acronym for Science, Technology, Engineering, and Mathematics, has recently been joined by Art to form STEAM. Is it really that important? Yes! Art is used to plan the layout of a tower, the design of a prosthetic hand, and the colors of the latest app. In fact, as long as your project is inquiry-based and you have the opportunity to think critically, creatively, and innovatively, then you are looking at a STEAM curriculum. Because the transition of terminology from STEM to STEAM is still tentative, we are using STEM for clarity's sake and listing art here separately in this handbook. But don't let that fool you into overlooking art this year. It really is a vital skill!

2020-2021 3rd-Grade Curriculum Handbook  •  800.478.0672

69

# DOODLE ADVENTURES: SLIMY SPACE SLUGS

~~BASIC~~ **COMPLETE ~ ELITE**

Some years ago the top buzzword for business was "creative." A few years later, the hot topic in education became creativity.

This trickle-down development should spur educators, especially those of us teaching at home, to look beyond easy "read-and-regurgitate" education that dulls the mind. Instead, we should lead a lifestyle that not only encourages imaginative efforts, but that also passionately carves out time for those pursuits every day.

The finest method we have found is both surprisingly easy and affordable – doodle books. A doodle a day has the potential to engage both sides of the brain and unleash a powerhouse of originality. And, with so much variety, it never gets old.

In Doodle Adventures: The Search for the Slimy Space Slugs, your child will join Carl, who is not only a duck, but also a member of a super-secret international group of explorers on a journey in search of a very important stolen artifact.

This delightful space-themed fantasy has your child draw himself into the story. Then, following prompts, he adds more illustrations and doodles as he locates the object, beats the bad guys, and gets his hero home safely. By the end of the book your child will have co-illustrated a hilarious book to share with family and friends.

Much more than a simple doodle book, Doodle Adventures: The Search for the Slimy Space Slugs is also a reading book with a quirky storyline. The completed book will make a great keepsake.

### Scheduling
This book has 105 pages in all; some are just for reading, and many feature doodling. For easiest scheduling, we suggest asking your child to complete 3 pages a week reading, doodling, or both as needed!

# PAINT-BY-NUMBER MUSEUM SERIES

~~BASIC~~ **COMPLETE ~ ELITE**

With the Paint-by-Number Museum Series, your young artist will get to imitate four very different famous masterpieces: The Eiffel Tower by Georges Seurat, The Starry Night by Vincent van Gogh, The Japanese Footbridge by Claude Monet, and Sunflowers by Vincent van Gogh.

Painting by number is often seen as being simplistic, uninspired, and mechanical. Yet Leonardo da Vinci himself assigned assistants to paint in numbered areas on a work that he had already sketched out. Completing paint-by-number projects helps your child learn to analyze a subject and observe areas of color, and it is an excellent exercise in brush control and strokes as he focuses entirely on getting the right color in the right spot.

Unlike other paint-by-number sets, the Paint-by-Number Museum Series does not print the numbers on each canvas, but rather on reference sheets so your artist can choose to imitate the masterpiece or paint with his own matchless style. Brief illustrated instructions with a snippet about the techniques used by the master artists when creating their works of art will get your miniaturist to the easel fast. The attention to detail and the skills developed are sure to set in motion a lifetime of art appreciation.

## Scheduling
With four paintings to complete, you could set these aside for special occasions or otherwise dreary weeks. Or, choose to allow your child to work on them a little bit every day until he has finished them!

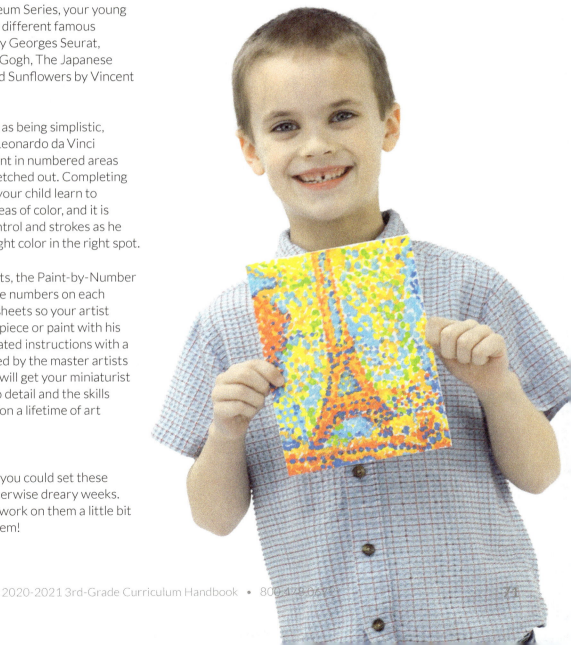

# ZENTANGLE FOR KIDS

## ~~BASIC~~ - COMPLETE ~ ELITE

Not only will your student love this book, he will actually walk away with transferable skills. Zentangle for Kids is an easy-to-learn, fun way to create striking images by drawing structured patterns.

What is the difference between a doodle and a Zentangle? Doodles are often random and done with no pre-planning. Zentangles are deliberate. The patterns each have a specific name and are built one pencil stroke at a time. By using concentration to complete a design, Zentangle for Kids intentionally facilitates a shift in focus while improving your child's eye-hand coordination and fine motor skills.

There are many Zentangle books available, but this one for children has the clearest instructions, the most motivating assignments, and is fully dogma-free. Enjoy.

For our most conservative customers: If the thought of Zen in the title scares you, bear this in mind–Zen in this context is not a way of thinking as much as a state of focus and concentration. Anyone who has ever cross-stitched a design, knitted an elaborate pattern, or calligraphed a verse has experienced that same deep-thinking, fully-focused condition with no scare of embracing Buddhism.

### Scheduling
Includes 43 spreads/activities, each with some wonderful complexity. Complete one to two a week, encouraging your child to take the time needed to do quality work.

# COMPLETE-A-SKETCH 123 CD

~~BASIC~ COMPLETE~~ ~ **ELITE**

Starting with simple incomplete drawings that need to be finished, this course will teach your child technical art skills.

Each page shows a small completed picture in the corner of the page. The balance of the page shows the same image with parts of the lines missing, but with critical intersections and line ends to define the image to be drawn.

Designed by a teaching dad for his home-taught son, these "technical art" lessons offer a great introduction to manual drafting.

With no formal teaching, your child will be motivated to take on his first drawings, and he will be rewarded with almost instant success.

Are you wondering if technical art is a worthwhile endeavor? The ability to draw in 2-D what you see in 3-D is something your child will use designing a chicken coop, sketching a raised vegetable bed, or illustrating a warm layette. Truly a valuable-for-a-lifetime skill!

To get the most use out of these, you'll want to help your child get to where he can replicate the drawing on a blank piece of paper. Here's what that may look like:

1. Complete the drawing using a ruler.
2. Complete the drawing with no ruler.
3. Mark a blank page with as many markings as you need to complete the drawing. (It may look similar to the page you started with on steps one and two.) Tracing is fine, but stay on this step until he can do it without tracing.
4. Complete the sketch on blank paper independently. (Your child may still make some guidemarks. That is normal,

as long as he can make them on the fly and keep going rather than agonizing over each one before he starts.)

## Scheduling

Includes 78 drawings, each designed to be repeated several times (see above) until your child can draw it with no assistance. Complete 2 to 3 drawings a week to mastery level and you'll easily finish this year.

## HOW DOES YOUR CHILD LEARN BEST?

Do you know your child's learning style? If not, you should take a few moments to research it. Once you know your child's strengths and weaknesses, you'll be able to focus on methods that actually help him learn instead of simply using the approach you've always used. (All learners usually find it helpful to integrate as many learning modes as possible into their studies.)

For instance, if you find you have a kinesthetic learner, allow and encourage him to move while he learns. Break out the Thinking Putty, let him sign keywords to himself, or write them on a whiteboard. If he's an auditory learner, make it a point to have him hear the information he's learning. You could read it to him, encourage him to read aloud, use an audio version, or download a podcast, but however you decide to approach it, he will be much better off than simply reading and re-reading the same textbook silently four dozen times. By the way, visual learners will probably find that they have the easiest time learning – after all, most information is naturally presented visually in any textbook.

# MIXED BY ME THINKING PUTTY

If you've been around Timberdoodle for long, you already know about our passion for Thinking Putty and the difference it can make for a fidgety student.

This kit takes that tool to a whole new level by encouraging your student to name and develop his very own custom putty. Want a little guidance? Try one of these ideas:

### Name It First
Have him come up with an idea first, then build the putty to suit. Perhaps he will want a putty that reminds him of scuba diving with Uncle Tim. Or perhaps he'd like to perfectly match the color of that gorgeous sunrise.

### It's a Theme!
He could name (or even develop) all five of the putties around a single theme. For instance, would you say the two completed ones shown on the previous page are jade and copper? Or are they perhaps seaweed and crab?

### Pro Tip
These tiny putties really only need a pinch of colors or special effects. As tempting as it will be to put in all of it, he may want to use only 1/5th of any add-in for a single tin until he has decided for sure that he doesn't want any of that add-in for the other four tins!

### Scheduling
Plan to make up at least one Thinking Putty in the first week of school. Completed putties are perfect for playing with while he watches his math lessons or at other times when his mind is more engaged than his hands.

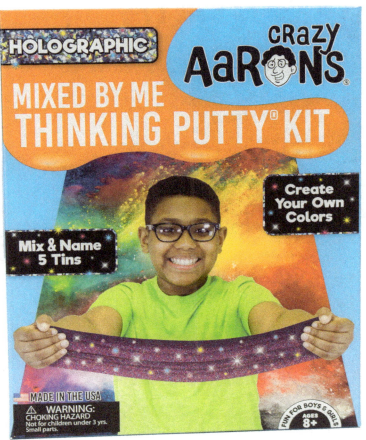

# TEST PREP

## ~~BASIC~~ COMPLETE ~ ELITE

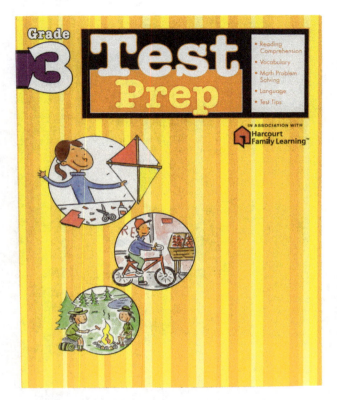

For those of us in a state where some form of testing is required, but never scrutinized, preparing is not as critical. But some of you are in states where the test results are not only analyzed but are used as a basis for whether you may continue to home educate. Why not make sure your children are "playing on a level playing field"? The Test Prep series offers students the essential groundwork needed to prepare for standardized tests.

Based on subject areas covered by most state standardized tests, these colorful, inviting workbooks provide a good sampling of all the skills required of each grade level. Practice pages, strategies, tips, and full-length practice tests build test-taking confidence and skills in subjects such as reading comprehension, vocabulary, language, and math. The test tips are beneficial, and the information and instructions are super-easy to follow. Developed by a leading educational publisher, Harcourt's Test Prep provides a great opportunity for children to review before taking standardized state tests. Engaging, practical, and easy to use, Test Prep will help your children face the tests with the same confidence that their peers will have.

Home-taught children who are not prepared for their yearly standardized tests are at a distinct disadvantage to the government- and privately-taught children. If you reside in a state that requires standardized tests, you should know that a vast majority of certified teachers teach with the test in mind. In other words, teachers understand the types of questions that will appear on the standardized tests, and they will spend weeks preceding the tests covering the necessary information. If you do not do likewise, your children stand a chance of performing poorly in comparison.

Even if your state doesn't require testing, consider completing the book anyway, since test-taking skills are vital across all areas of life.

### Scheduling

Our family has always preferred to spend the week or two before our state-mandated annual testing working through this book. Keep it low key, and let the change of pace be an enjoyable experience for your child. If you run into a concept he doesn't know, stop and explain it to him; that is why you are doing the prep now!

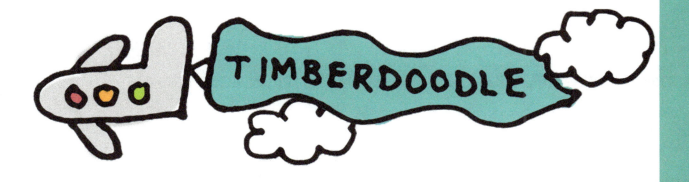

## FROM OUR FAMILY TO YOURS

In 1986 we were a family of five. I was the oldest of three toddler girls with a mom who absolutely excelled at educating us at home. Of course, this was during "The Dark Ages" of homeschooling, and online searching was still a thing of the future. Our mom, Deb, was (and is) a voracious reader, though, and an avid researcher. We girls were thriving academically and, naturally, other moms were interested in using the same curricula Deb had found.

So, in 1986 she and Dan, our dad, repurposed the business license originally intended for their world-class Golden Retriever breeding operation (which had come to naught), and she launched Timberdoodle, a homeschool supply company. A catalog was born, and growth came fast. We shipped from our laundry room, the grandparents' basement, and finally, warehouses and an office. Two more children were added, and all of us grew up working in the business from an early age.

Now, decades later, Timberdoodle is still renowned for out-of-the-box learning and crazy-smart finds. Mom's engineering background has heavily influenced our STEM selections, and her no-nonsense, independent approach has made these kits the award-winning choice that they are today.

All five of us are grown now, and most still work at Timberdoodle in key roles. Abel and his wife are homeschooling their young ones, while my sisters and I have opened our lives to fostering children. The kits we sell are the same ones we use in our own homes, and we hope you enjoy them as much as we do.

In the following articles, you'll hear from Deb and others about some of the nitty-gritty questions we often field. Do you have a question not answered here? Don't forget that you are invited to contact us at any time—we'd love to help!

Joy (for all of us)

# WHAT MAKES GAMES A PRIORITY?

**6 REASONS GAMES AREN'T JUST FOR FUN, EVEN THE "FRIVOLOUS" GAMES**

You may have noticed that this year there is at least one multi-player game in every curriculum kit. This is not just to add some levity to your day!

**The Research**
A quick google search will net you numbers of articles on the benefits of playing board games iwith your children. Here are just some of those benefits:

- increasing laughter
- language development
- understanding rules
- grasping fair play
- detecting patterns and predicting outcomes
- learning from experience
- impulse control

- social skills
- increasing focus
- teamwork
- reducing anxiety
- unplugging from technology
- increasing analytical abilities
- setting goals
- patience
- problem solving skills
- reducing stress
- creativity
- prioritizing steps towards a goal
- self-confidence
- spatial ability

This is a robust and interwoven list, but here are the five things that have jumped out at us over the past year and made this a huge priority for your child's education.

**1. Social-Emotional Intelligence**
Think of your closest and dearest friends outside of your immediate family. What makes them so dear to you? My guess is that it isn't their IQ or ability to speed solve a complex math problems. A friendship will celebrate those interesting facts, but your friendship itself is more likely rooted in shared interests, time spent, and an ability to navigate hard situations with grace.

When you spend time teaching a child how to lose graciously, you are teaching a life skill that will translate into all of life and impact their friendships way more than their test scores ever could.

In light of this the end of each game may be more important than the strategy in the middle. Coach your children in what you expect from the winner and the loser. Around here, a "Good game!" goes a long way but you decide what is best for your family. Humility is what you're looking to see. Not the teary deflation of a proud loser or the puffed up bragging of a proud winner!

## 2. Strategic Thinking
Obviously, the games we've chosen require age-appropriate logic and strategy. Critical thinking skills are essential, so let's teach them any way we may.

## 3. Connection
It can seem that as your children get older your parenting gets more and more hands-off. Or, for a younger child, it may seem that you spend more time correcting behaviour than you do connecting with your child. Making games a priority lets you enjoy each other's company and genuinely become closer to each other. What parent won't appreciate that?

## 4. Executive Functioning
Are you familiar with executive functioning? It is the ability to prioritize and organize information. The clearest example we've been given is the age old challenge to "guess what number I'm thinking of right now using yes or no questions". If you respond by asking if the number is higher than 100, you are using executive functioning. If instead you start rattling off numbers, you're not. In games you're constantly taking into consideration what your opponent is doing, what pieces are still in your hand, which rules apply at the

moment... and sorting/utilizing all the information to decide what your next game play should be.

## 5. Regulation
Some articles tie this to executive fuctioning, but it's worth discussing on its own. Regulation is the ability to control your own emotions - can you think of a more natural opportunity to practice this than during game play? Calm-down strategies and redos may be implemented as many times as needed, until your child is able to endure suspense and even win our lose without outbursts. Phew!

## 6. Growth Mindset
Yes, this is a buzzword right now, but it is worth mentioning. Some of us, students included, tend to think that we are good at something or we're not. For our PreK twins this has been particularly obvious in our discussions about art. One has a natural inclination for drawing and one does not. So the naturally gifted one calls himself an artist and proclaims that his brother is not. It is helpful to come back and discuss that we all learn and grow. So when Mr. Artist set aside his art for several months and his twin worked and worked at it, we had two artists on our hands! Gameplay is a natural place to model that all of us learn and grow in our skill sets. You aren't simply "born with it" but you learn skills and develop abilities.

## Side Note: Think Out Loud
An article from Parenting Science made an excellent point that student's don't always naturally ask why a player used a specific strategy. Try to start that conversation by asking why he chose to _ or explain that you're starting with this piece because _. This will model the higher order thinking that you are setting out to teach. It will also model the fact that we are all learners here!

So what are you waiting for? Go play some games!

# WHY EMPHASIZE INDEPENDENT LEARNING?

**THE TOP SEVEN REASONS THIS IS SUCH A BIG DEAL AT TIMBERDOODLE**

### 1. Avoid Burn Out

One-on-one teaching is critical to the success of any student, and homeschoolers are no exception to that. However, we have seen moms who become helicopter moms, micromanaging every detail of their students' education. Is it any wonder that these moms burn out? Independent learning tools provide a natural transition from the one-on-one of early childhood to a less mom-intense educational approach.

### 2. Cultivate Responsible Learners

There is a lot of (dare we say it?) fun in teaching. But it is better for your students if they master how to learn on their own. After all, when they are adults, you'll want them to have the ability to pick up any skill they want and learn it as needed. Structuring their education to be more and more self-taught helps them to become responsible self-learners.

### 3. Special Needs, Illness, and Newborns

Not all moms have the same amount of teaching time. Whether they are doing therapy for a child with autism, dealing with their own chronic illness, managing visits for a foster child, or are blessed with a newborn, there are seasons when homeschooling needs to be more independent simply for mom's sanity!

### 4. You Don't Have to Love Teaching

As much as no one wants to mention this, we all know moms who really struggle to teach. They love their kids and feel strongly about homeschooling, but when it actually comes down to teaching they are easily overwhelmed and intimidated. If it is an area they are not gifted/trained in, then of course teaching is scary. Independent learning tools can help get them comfortable in their role, but even if they never love teaching they can still reap the benefits of giving their children a superior education at home.

### 5. Timberdoodle's Purpose: We Are Here to Make Giving Your Children a Superior Education at Home Enjoyable

Here at Timberdoodle, amid the catalogs, sales, blog posts, videos, Facebook giveaways, etc., we have one primary goal. That goal is to make it possible for parents to enjoy giving their children a superior education at home. We aren't here to sell you stuff (though we wouldn't exist if you didn't shop!), which is why we have been known to send you to our "competitors" when their product would work better for you. We really just want you to be a happy homeschool family. When that happens, we feel successful! Independent learning is one tool in your toolbox. It is a valuable tool, so use it where it works best for you.

### 6. Not Either/Or

You don't have to pick between independent and group learning across the board. Take The Fallacy Detective, for instance. It is designed for a student to pick up and read independently. Instead, our family did it as a read-aloud and took turns answering the questions. The result? Not only did we have a blast, but we were also all on the same page regarding logical fallacies. Bumper stickers and ads we came

across in daily life were fodder for vigorous discussions about the underlying fallacies in ways that would never have happened if we each studied it alone. So even if you're striving to teach independent learning, don't hesitate to do some things together!

### 7. Our Family

The rule of thumb in our house was that as soon as a child could read, he or she was responsible for his or her own education. We each had an annual conference with Mom to set learning goals for the year, then we were given the books for the year, often including the teacher's manuals. Mom gave us each a weekly checklist to complete before Friday Family Night. If we needed help, we were to ask for it. Otherwise, the responsibility was ours. This freed us up to do the truly important things (devotions, service, Timberdoodle work, babysitting, elder care, church projects, hospitality, farming...) as a family.

# 9 REASONS TO STOP SCHOOLWORK AND GO BUILD SOMETHING!

Would you like to supplement your curriculum with a program that simultaneously improves your child's visual perception, fine motor skills, patience, problem solving, spatial perception, creativity, ability to follow directions, grasp of physics concepts, and engineering ability? Better yet, what if your child would actually enjoy this curriculum and choose to do it whenever he could? No, this isn't some mythical homeschool product guaranteed to solve all your problems for a large fee—we are talking about the LEGO® bricks already strewn throughout your house, the blocks in our preschool curriculum, and the Bioloid robot kit designed for teens.

Construction kits just might be the most underrated type of curriculum ever. It's not just us; research concludes that children learn a lot by designing and building things. Based on our own engineering background/bias, we believe that construction is one of the most valuable educational processes available. For that reason, both learning to build and learning by what has been built should be a part of every family's curriculum. Here are our top nine skills your child will learn with his construction kit:

### 1. Visual Perception
It may be obvious that it takes visual perception to find the right pieces and place them well, but consider that whether your child is reading, finishing a puzzle, or doing open-heart surgery, a proficiency in visual perception is mandatory!

## 2. Fine Motor Skills

Boys especially seem to struggle with fine motor skills, particularly when it comes to writing and drawing. Amazingly enough, though, they are often the most passionate about building—the natural remedy! The more they fine-tune their dexterity, the easier "school time" becomes for both of you!

## 3. Patience

Do you know anyone who couldn't stand to be a little more patient? Construction takes time. Slowing down, reading the directions, doing it over when a piece has been placed wrong or a sibling knocks over your creation… these are all valuable character-building experiences!

## 4. Problem Solving

Some children simply lack the ability to troubleshoot a situation and figure out the next step. Construction sets provide a structured opportunity to figure out what went wrong and fix it, if you're following the directions. If you are designing your own models, you'll have even more opportunities to problem solve!

## 5. Spatial Perception

Probably the clearest picture of how important it is to be able to mentally convert 2-D images into 3-D objects is that of a surgeon. Knowing where the spleen is on a 2-D textbook page isn't nearly the same thing as being able to reach into an incision and find the damaged spleen!

## 6. Creativity

Not every creative person has artistic ability. But construction can open the doors of creativity like no other tool. What if I move this gear over here? Could I build that bridge with only blue pieces?

## 7. Following Directions

Some children are natural rule followers and need to be encouraged to be creative. Others need to constrain themselves to follow directions, at least on occasion! If your child falls into that camp, construction kits are a natural way to encourage him in this skill, with the added benefit of a finished result he can show off!

## 8. Grasp of Physics

Friction, force, mass, and energy are all basic physics concepts much more easily explained and grasped with a set of blocks and a ball than simply by studying a dry textbook definition!

## 9. Engineering Ability

Many "born engineers" are not drawn to textbooks. But set a construction kit in front of them and watch them explore pulleys, levers, wheels, and gears. They'll soon go from exploration to innovation, and you'll be amazed at their inventions!

# WHAT IF THIS IS TOO HARD?

## 9 STEPS TO TAKE IF YOU'RE FEELING OVERWHELMED

Everyone has felt overwhelmed at some point in his or her education. Whether it's a groan from you as you pull a giant textbook out of the box or the despair from your child when he's read the directions five times and the robot STILL isn't operating as he wants it to, you will almost certainly hit a moment this year when you realize that an aspect of homeschooling is harder than you anticipated.

So, what do you do now?

### 1. Take a Breath
Just knowing that everyone faces this should help you relax a bit. This feeling will not last–you'll get through this!

### 2. Jump In!
Why are you stressed right now? Are you stressed because "it" is so intimidating that you haven't been quite ready to dive into it? If that's the case, the simplest solution is to jump in and get started. Could you read the first page together before lunch? What if you have your student find all of the pieces for step one today? Sometimes it's better to muddle through a lesson together than to wait until you're ready to teach it perfectly.

### 3. Step Back
Perhaps you're too close right now. If you're mid-project with incredible effort and totally frustrated by how it's going, try the opposite approach. Close the book for 30 minutes (set a timer!) and go grab lunch, hit the playground, or swap to a more hands-on project. When the timer rings, you and your student will be ready to try again with clearer heads.

### 4. Time This
Timers are an invaluable learning tool. If you're being distracted, try setting a 10- or 20-minute timer during which you'll do only _____. Or tell yourself you definitely need to tackle That Dreaded Subject, but only for 30 minutes a day, in two 15-minute chunks. When the timer rings, close the text and move to the next thing. Dividing your day into blocks of time can make a remarkable difference in your efficiency level.

### 5. Level Down
Did your student take the math placement test before jumping in this year? Perhaps he is just in the wrong level! If moving to an easier level kind of freaks you out, it may help to remember that you and your student are not defined by his skill set in any field, and faking his way through by blood, sweat, and tears does not help his future self. Taking the time to back up and fill in the gaps, though, that will benefit him forever!

### 6. Simplify
If you are trying to do every possible activity in every course, it's no wonder you're exhausted. By the time your student is in high school, he will need to complete 75% or more of the work in each course to get full credits. We're not advocates of doing the work in name only, but it's okay to watch some experiments online rather than completing each one in the

dining room. It's also appropriate to only do every other math problem in a section if your child is bored to tears with yet another page of addition. Doesn't that feel better?

### 7. Make Accommodations
What exactly is stressing your student (or you!) out right now? Is it the pen-to-paper writing component? Why not let him use the computer and type his work instead? Or perhaps he can dictate to you while you write for him. Make sure you're doing whatever you can to engage his best learning style. Encourage Mr. Auditory Learner to read aloud if necessary. Or break out all of the favorite fidgets and let Miss Kinesthetic work at a standing desk.

### 8. Get Help
Ask another teacher/parent to take some time working through the issue with you. You may be surprised by how much clarity you gain with a fresh set of eyes. (Our Facebook groups can be great for this!)

### 9. Get Professional Help
Check the publisher's website, the book's teacher page, or the kit's manual for contact information. Most of the authors and manufacturers we work with are fantastic about helping and coaching those who get stuck. Not getting the help you need from them? Contact mail@Timberdoodle.com or call us at 800–478–0672 and we'll work with them to get that answer for you.

# 9 TIPS FOR HOMESCHOOLING GIFTED CHILDREN

### 1. Disdain Busywork

Your child wants to learn, so don't slow him down! If he has mastered multiplication, why are you still spending an hour a day reviewing it? Yes, he does need some review, but we've seen way too many families focus on completing every problem rather than mastering the material. One way to test this is to have him try doing only every other review problem and see how he does. If he can prove he's mastered it, he doesn't need to be spending quite as much time on it.

### 2. Go Deep

Allow breathing room in your schedule so you have time to investigate earth's gravitational pull or the advantages/disadvantages of hair sheep vs. woolly sheep. Remember that your child is asking to learn, so why pull him away from the subject that's fascinating him? After all, we all know that material we're interested in sticks with us so much better than things we learn only because we must.

### 3. Go Fast

If your child wants to take three science courses this year or race through two math levels, then why not let him? Homeschoolers can absolutely rock this because there are no peers holding them to a "traditional" pace!

### 4. Encourage Completion

Sometimes I think there is a touch of ADD in every genius. Give your child as much flexibility as you possibly can, but also keep in mind that you'll be doing him a disservice if he never has to tackle something he doesn't feel like working on at the moment. Sometimes he may even be surprised to realize that the very subject he dreaded is the springboard for a whole new area of investigation!

### 5. Give Space & Opportunities

If you can keep mandatory studies to a minimum, you'll give your child more opportunities to accelerate his learning in the areas he's gifted at. Common sense, perhaps, but also worth deliberately thinking through as you plan out your school year.

## 6. Work on Weak Areas Carefully

While you definitely want to work with him to help him overcome areas he's just not as strong in, you also want to be careful that a weakness in one area doesn't impede his progress in other ways. For instance, a child may struggle with writing simply because his brain works much faster than his hands. While I encourage such a family to work on handwriting skills, I also suggest that they try teaching their child to type and allow him to complete writing assignments on the computer. This lets him continue to build his writing skills instead of holding him back because of his lack of handwriting speed.

## 7. Emphasize Humility & Service

We have met way too many children who are obnoxiously convinced that they are geniuses and that everyone needs to be in awe of their abilities. Your child will be much healthier (and happier!) if he realizes these four things:

- His identity is NEVER found in his brainpower.

- Even as gifted as he is, there are still things that others do better than he does.

- He is much more than his brain. (Should he lose his "edge," he won't lose his worth!)

- His gifts are not for himself alone but for serving God and His people.

Of course, the goal is never to insult or degrade him but to give him a framework from which he can truly thrive and be free to learn. With a proper perspective, he'll be able to enjoy learning without the burden of constantly assessing his genius and worrying what people will think of him. Don't weigh him down by constantly telling him how big his brain is, either. Encourage his learning, but don't forget to cultivate his character at all costs. In 10 years, his response to rebuke will be much more telling than his test score this year, so don't put an inordinate stress on intellectual pursuits.

## 8. Talk a LOT!

Talk about what he's interested in. Talk about the theories he came up with today. Talk about his daydreams. Talk about what he wants to study up on. Talk about why he may actually need to master that most-dreadful-of-subjects, whatever that may be to him... Not only will you be able to impart your years of wisdom to him, but you'll also know well the subjects he's interested in and be able to tie those in to his other studies, the places you're visiting next week, or that interesting article you read yesterday.

## 9. Relax!

Your child is a wonderful gift; don't feel that every moment must be spent maximizing his potential. As a side benefit, just relaxing about his genius may in fact increase it. Our own family found that some of our best test scores came after a year off of most formal schooling! Not what we would have planned, but a very valuable insight. Living life=learning, so maximize that!

# CONVERGENT & DIVERGENT THINKING

Have you considered the necessity of incorporating both convergent and divergent thinking into your learning time? Experts recognize these as the two major types of brain challenges we all encounter.

Does that just sound like a whole bunch of big words? No worries, let's break it down. Your child needs to be able to find the right answer when needed (math, medicine dosage) and also needs to be able to come up with a creative, unscripted answer when the situation warrants (art, architecture...).

A child who can only find the "right" answer will be a rigid thinker who can't problem-solve well or think outside the box.

A child who only thinks creatively will not be able to follow procedures or do anything that involves math.

## What Is Convergent Thinking?

To go more in-depth, convergent thinking generally involves finding a single best answer and is important in the study of math and science. Convergent thinking is the backbone of the majority of curricula and is crucial for future engineers, doctors, and even parents. Much of daily life is a series of determining right and wrong answers, and standardized tests favor the convergent thinker. But when we pursue only convergent-rich curricula we miss the equally vital arena of divergent thinking.

## Is Divergent Thinking Different?

Yes! Divergent thinking encourages your child's mind to explore many possible solutions, maybe even ideas that aren't necessarily apparent at first. It is in use when he discovers that there is more than one way to build a bridge with blocks, to animate a movie, or even simply to complete a doodle. Radically different from read-and-regurgitate textbooks, divergent activities are not only intellectually stimulating, but kids love them, too.

## Make a Conscious Effort to Include Both in Your Curriculum

Admittedly, because most textbooks and even puzzles are designed for convergent thinking, you will need to make a conscious effort to expose your children to multiple opportunities for divergent thinking. It is imperative because both divergent and convergent thinking are necessary for critical thinking to be effective.

## Why Doctors Need Both Skills

As an example, let's look at a medical doctor. A physician needs to be extraordinarily skilled at convergent thinking to dose medications correctly, diagnose life-threatening

emergencies, and follow safety procedures to avoid infection. However, the first person to wash his hands before surgery or to find a treatment for Ebola used divergent thinking. Some of the best doctors today are those who employ powerful convergent skills to accurately diagnose, paired with curiosity and divergent thinking to find the most effective or previously undiscovered treatment plans.

## Convergent in Third Grade?

From reading to math, the backbone of your curriculum this year is convergent. This makes sense, because so much of learning at this level is simply marveling at facts. Sometimes there really is a right answer!

## Is Divergent in Third Grade?

These tools all include strong divergent potential to help your child become a well-rounded thinker:

- **Möbi Max**
- **GraviTrax Deluxe Set**
- **Anomia Kids**
- **Scratch Coding Cards**
- **Doodle Adventures**
- **Zentangle for Kids**

Several of these actually do both aspects well. For instance, when your child is recreating the Scratch programs as instructed, that's a convergent skill. But when he develops his own versions or uses his entire repertoire to create a new program in Scratch, that's divergent thinking! Even Möbi Max transforms the convergent skill of mathematics to a divergent skill as your child adjusts and rearranges equations to use all of his tiles.

# WHY ISN'T THERE A BIBLE COURSE?

## OUR FAVORITE BIBLE TOOLS, 4 WAYS WE'VE DONE DEVOTIONS, AND MORE

From the time our children could sit in our laps, family devotion was a mainstay in our home, so teaching Bible to our children was paramount. But for too many families the sum total of Bible instruction for their children is Bible workbooks that are little more than read-and-regurgitate exercises, and that alarms me. Yes, we do want children to know the facts of the Bible – who killed a giant with a small stone, who was thrown into a lion's den, and who changed water into wine–and resources such as The Action Bible do a splendid job of teaching those facts. But my experience has been that children need massive amounts of intimate daily input to fully grasp the glory of the gospel, and there is no easier way than through daily family devotions.

### Then What About Requiring Children to Read Their Bibles Every Day?

That is certainly the trajectory we all want for our children, but how is that working for you personally? Have you ever had times where you "read" your daily chapter(s) while thinking about dinner, the toddler meltdown, or updating your shopping list? Your children have the same struggles.

### How Is a Daily Devotional Different?

With a daily devotional, the Bible reading can be explored in a much more personal manner. You know your child better than any publisher, and if the prescribed questions are not relevant to the sins and follies of your child, you can adapt and even drill down further. You can also use that time to point out how the Word is living and active in your own life with personal anecdotes that pertain to the topic at hand.

### Then Can't You Include Devotional Materials with Each Grade Level?

No, for the simple reason that many of our favorite devotional materials, in particular Long Story Short and Old Story New, are usable for multiple ages and multiple years. And because God's work in each family is unique, we are much more comfortable exposing you to what we consider the best all-around resources and letting you cherry pick the most appropriate for your use and your situation.

### What Does the Ideal Devotional Look Like?

We are ardent proponents of reading the Bible every day. For the little ones there is the The Big Picture Story Bible, slightly older ones will enjoy The Jesus Storybook Bible, and then they should be ready for Long Story Short and Old Story New. But don't stop there; add in great theological books that you have enjoyed. When our children were little we read books by John Piper, Ravi Zacharias, R.C. Sproul, Randy Alcorn, and Martyn Lloyd-Jones. We read them slowly, sometimes just a page or two a day, pausing often to discuss the concepts and how they related to our lives, the lives of their friends, and the world at large. Every devotional time ended with a chapter out of a true-to-life story, both Christian and secular, where opportunities again presented themselves to discuss motivations, temptations, and how God's Word pertains to this situation.

### Do You Have Specific Recommendations for Third Grade?

We are big fans of:

What Every Child Should Know About Prayer

The Jesus Storybook Bible

The Biggest Story

Long Story Short

Old Story New

The Gospel Story Bible

Indescribable

Thoughts to Make Your Heart Sing

Cat & Dog Theology

Exploring the Bible

Big Beliefs

Wise Up

The Radical Book for Kids

The Action Bible

The Ology: Ancient Truths Ever New...

And that's just the highlights! To see our most current favorites, just pop by the website. (Also, keep in mind that if you have reward points on file, this could be a wonderful way to use them.)

## What Do Your Family Devotions Really Look Like?

As you can imagine, this shifts dramatically over time. Let me give you four different snap shots from recent years:

### 2016: Herding Cats

As a foster family with little ones 1–4 years old, devotion time has radically changed from previous years when we were a family of grown-ups!

Our morning devotion routine starts with gathering the family and getting the little ones seated quietly on the couch. Honestly, this is probably the most difficult part! Some mornings are (finally!) almost effortless, but some mornings way more time is spent on obedience than on devotions. Not to worry, this is both normal and extraordinarily valuable for the children. In fact, the toddlers probably benefit more from that training than from the actual contents of devotion time.

Once everyone is seated, we briefly review yesterday's lesson and read a new page from *Everything a Child Should Know About God*. We're loving this book for our current little ones as it covers the basics in a paragraph or two every day–perfect for tiny attention spans!

We then do our memory verse of the week. Right now we're using Foundation Fighter Verses to help us select meaningful texts, and we're setting every verse to ASL sign. We're all learning and signing it together, keeping everyone engaged.

Finally, we end with a simple song, again with sign language. On occasion we've found a YouTube video showing other kids singing and signing, and that's always a bonus. But we've found that just learning it together works well also, and that gives us a much broader selection of songs to pick from.

# WHY ISN'T THERE A BIBLE COURSE? CONT.

All told, this is probably a 5- to 10-minute process. While more could be added (I'm eager to add more catechism components as one of our kids loves those), we're very excited to see our little ones learning the story line and theology of the Bible in a way that they enjoy.

In the evening we watch another chapter from *The Jesus Storybook Bible* DVDs together just before tucking our little ones in for the night. Much of it goes over their heads, but it is a wonderful way to end the day for all of us.

## 2017: Including Aspects from Church

Our little ones are now ages 2.5 to almost 5, and our morning devotions have shifted slightly.

Our main lesson now comes from *The Beginner's Gospel Story Bible*. It is as vibrant and interesting as our little ones are, and it does a wonderful job of presenting the gospel as seen throughout the Bible.

Our church uses *The Gospel Project*, so we end our morning

devotions with this week's Big Picture Q & A, memory verse, and song. The familiarity of hearing the exact same thing at church on Sunday is really good for our children, and it's good for us, too!

This is still probably a 5- to 10-minute process. While more could be

added, we're very excited to see our little ones learning the story line and theology of the Bible in a way that they enjoy.

We've already switched our evening devotions to an advent theme, since we have high ambitions for their Christmas memory work. Each child is invited to hold a (battery operated!) candle and clutch a stuffed goat (from "the shepherd's flock") while we all sing a handful of Christmas carols and then recite the Christmas story from Luke 2. It is a wonderful way to end the day for all of us!

## 2018: Advent

We're forgoing a formal morning routine now, and instead whoever is working with the kids on any particular morning gets some Bible time in with them, in whatever format works best for them (rereading a Bible book, modifying a Sunday school curriculum, etc...).

Our oldest child is also doing Bible time during her daily school time with Aunt Pearl, who has a routine adapted from *Exploring the Bible* where she reads portions of the Scripture as the five-year-old does her STEM work or other hands-only work. They then highlight what they've read to mark their progress. This child struggles with auditory processing, so Pearl is always working to fine-tune the method and make it work for her.

At night, though, we all gather and light the Advent candles. (We chose the Advent Wreath with a new candle every day.) We then sing an increasing number of Christmas carols, adding a new one every week, and recite a chunk of Luke 2 together. We end with a small chocolate for all participants.

This is a change of pace from our regular routine, and it

allows us all to absorb more of the wonders of the season together.

## 2020: Gratitude and Chaos

Our five little ones now range from babies to a five-year-old, and we're finding that we need to be punctual in our routine or the chaos ensues quickly.

The morning and school routines remain unchanged for now, and evening is when the formal Bible time happens.

After everyone is in his or her jammies and ready for bed, we sing a hymn of the week together. No one is reading yet, so we choose hymns with repetition and themes that will be relevant. (We're by no means a hymns-only family, but there is a richness in hymns that we so want our little ones to taste.)

We then read a chapter from *The Beginner's Gospel Story Bible* together, usually while the reader and the little ones sprawl all over the floor. We've done this book before, but it's been long enough that the kids are enjoying the repetition and getting more out of it this time through.

Once that is done, the "big kids" (ages 3–5) grab their gratitude journals and adult buddies, and together we write and draw something they are grateful for about the day. (The child dictates, we scribe and illustrate.) This is a concept we're still working to cement in their minds, but it is so valuable to both help their brains retain memories and to help them see every good gift as coming from God.

The kids reconvene in the living room a few minutes later for a chapter from a just-for-fun bedtime story.

## So What's Your Plan?

This year has the potential for rich and vibrant growth in your child's life. Don't put off making any decisions or you'll end the year right where you started. We'd encourage you to jump in and try something. Not working well? Tweak it! Find the best time of day, content, and format for your family right now, and don't be afraid to make changes as needed.

# HELP! MY BOOK SAYS "COMMON CORE!"

## THE TRUTH ABOUT WHETHER YOUR TIMBERDOODLE CURRICULUM KIT IS ALIGNED WITH COMMON CORE

There's been a lot of buzz, discussion, and anxiety in the homeschool community for the last decade about the Common Core State Standards. Many of you have asked us what our stance is on the standards and whether our curriculum is designed to comply with them.

### What Is the Common Core?

According to the CCSS website, "The Common Core State Standards Initiative is a state-led effort that established a single set of clear educational standards for kindergarten through 12th grade in English language arts and mathematics that states voluntarily adopt."

### But Isn't That a Good Idea?

Growing up as an Air Force "brat," Deb, Timberdoodle's founder, attended many different schools throughout her educational career. She can tell you just how much easier it would have been for her if all of the schools covered the same materials in the same order. Then, she could transfer effortlessly between them instead of missing critical information because the new school had already covered something her old school hadn't addressed yet. So, yes, the concept may be brilliant, but there are some very valid concerns.

### Why Homeschoolers Are Concerned

There is some real concern in the homeschooling community about what the Common Core Standards Initiative will mean to our families. In an early article posted by the Homeschool Legal Defense Association, HSLDA Director of Federal Relations William Estrada wrote, "The CCSS specifically do not apply to private or homeschools... However, HSLDA has serious concerns with the rush to adopt the CCSS. HSLDA has fought national education standards for the past two decades. Why? National standards lead to national curriculum and national tests, and subsequent pressure on homeschool students to be taught from the same curricula."

## Declining Quality?

Some in the homeschooling community have also expressed concern that as curriculum publishers endeavor to align with the CCSS, the educational quality in those texts will actually decrease rather than improve, while some are disenchanted with the atypical teaching methods employed by the CCSS, among other concerns.

## What We Are Doing

At Timberdoodle, our approach is simple. We are ignoring the CCSS and continuing to search out crazy-smart curricula, exactly what we've been doing for the past 30+ years. Our specialty has always been hand-picking the best products in every subject area and offering the families who trust us the same products we have used or would happily use ourselves. And we have no plans to change the way we carefully review every resource we sell.

## Some Products Do Say Common Core

Some of the items in this kit do, in fact, align with the CCSS. Not because we've sought that out, but because the quality resources we've chosen for our curriculum are already up to that standard or beyond. It is no surprise to us that the excellent tools we are excited about are also good enough to exceed the qualifications for the CCSS.

## This Has Never Changed and Will Not Change Now

At Timberdoodle, we work with trusted publishers and products we review carefully, not just in math and language arts but in all subject areas, so that we feel confident we are providing some of the best resources available for your children. Every time an item we've loved is revised (or stamped Common Core), we make sure that it has not been watered down or made confusing. Our goal is to exceed educational requirements, not by aligning our curriculum with any government standard, but by continuing to find products that work well and meet the high standards we hold for our families and yours.

# MOSDOS OPAL WEEKLY ASSIGNMENTS

## A SAMPLE DETAILED SCHEDULE

Here's one way to break down your assignments to flow easily through a 36-week schedule.

The page numbers refer to the current student reader as of this printing.

You'll notice that some weeks have more titles assigned than others. We've taken into account the number of corresponding workbook pages and the length of the readings to come up with these weekly assignments, but you should always feel free to rearrange in whatever fashion works for you. The surrounding content (e.g. introductory matter or sidebars) varies too, and your mathematically inclined student will quickly notice that no two weeks have identical page counts. Remind him that this is a good time to learn how to be flexible and persistent. After all, he may even find that the longer stories end up being his favorites!

Please note that you only need to complete as many of the corresponding activity pages and assignments as you determine to be appropriate for your reader. Our family would have chosen to answer the Studying the Selection questions in the readers orally rather than in writing. We would also likely skip the writing assignments since you'll be covering writing systematically with Daily 6-Trait Writing.

### SUGGESTED WEEK-BY-WEEK PLAN
**BOOK 1 SUNFLOWER**
**UNIT 1**
**All About the Story!**

### WEEK 1
Lesson in Literature... What Is a Story? - page 2
The Jar of Tassai - page 4
The Secret - page 16
Activity pages and assignments.

### WEEK 2
Lesson in Literature... What Is Plot? - page 18
The Story of the White Sombrero - page 20
Activity pages and assignments.

**UNIT 2**
**All About the Plot!**

**UNIT 3**
**All About the Characters!**

# MOSDOS OPAL WEEKLY ASSIGNMENTS CONTINUED, WEEKS 12-30

**BOOK 2 DAISY**
**UNIT 4**
**All About Setting!**

Now celebrate! You've made your way through a very rich year's study of literature!

# 584 BOOK SUGGESTIONS

So you love the idea of the reading challenge, but you'd like a boost to get you started? You've come to the right place!

## Customize This!
You'll find a few ideas here for each challenge, but don't forget that you're not bound to our list. There are literally hundreds more options that may be even better for your family. Use these pages as starter ideas and not as your final list.

## Will I See the Same Books Over and Over?
No, not on this list! However, you can expect to see some of these books appear on the lists for more than one grade (so if you have a third-grader and a fourth-grader, some parts of the list will match), since books are often appropriate for more than one grade level.

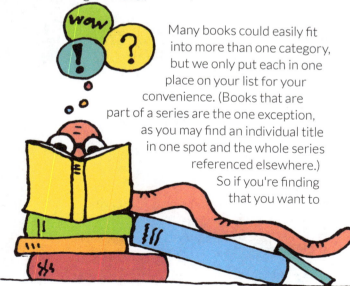

Many books could easily fit into more than one category, but we only put each in one place on your list for your convenience. (Books that are part of a series are the one exception, as you may find an individual title in one spot and the whole series referenced elsewhere.) So if you're finding that you want to

read more than one book from a particular challenge, the odds are good that skimming the list will give you another challenge to list it under. For instance, *Heidi*, from challenge 10 (a book more than 100 years old), would also fit really well under challenge 12 (a book about relationships or friendship), challenge 45 (a book about a girl), or challenge 88 (a book set in Europe). Shuffle things as you like!

## Repeated Authors
In this grade you'll find a lot of Boxcar Children, Mr. Putter & Tabby, Flat Stanley, Nancy Clancy, etc. Not a fan? Just skip them! But most kids love the repetition of finding the same heroes in a new story, so we have not hesitated to include much of the series throughout the challenges when appropriate.

## A Variety of Reading Levels
Some of these books are clearly geared as a read-aloud at this age and would be challenging for most third-graders to read independently. However, most of the books do fall into the range of material typically suggested for a third-grader. Our suggestion would be not to worry much about which books are read by your student vs. yourself. Grab the titles that interest you and him, and then flip through them. Which is he ready to enjoy reading? Set those aside for him. The rest you'll read to him. As your year progresses and his skills increase, you'll likely find you are setting more and more books aside for him to read. Read-alouds meet your child's tremendous need for literacy, language, and stories, though, so never shy away from simply reading to him!

## A Note About Our Book Ideas
If you've been reading to your child long (or if you've simply

perused your local public library), you've probably noticed that families have very different standards for their reading materials. The books you'll find listed here are ones that members of our team have read, have added to their "I want to read this" list, or have had recommended to them.

Even among our team there is a wide range in what titles our families would find acceptable. Some of us find fantasy objectionable and would skip books that obscure a solid Christian worldview but will gladly read a scarier adventure story than other families would be comfortable with. Others of us consider those fantasy titles to be an interesting addition and worthy of much discussion. We've opted to include titles with abandon, knowing that you will be able to flip through them at the library to determine if they are a good fit for your family.

**So this is not a "Timberdoodle would sell these books if we could" list.** We can't vouch for each of the titles, and we certainly can't know which ones are a good fit for your particular family. Mostly we're providing this list to give you some ideas, just in case you're drawing a blank in thinking of books for a particular topic. Use these ideas as the jumping-off point for which they are intended, and, as always, we highly recommend previewing the books yourself.

## Use Your Library

We can't overemphasize how useful your local library will be to you this year. We've listed multiple options under each challenge to try to ensure at least one title will be available. Now that most libraries allow you to place books on hold online, you'll find that you can use any spare hour in your day to request books for the next challenges and then whoever is in town next can swing by the library and pick them up. If you've not yet become a dedicated library user, this is the year!

## Reading and Talking

If you're newer to reading together, our biggest tips for you are these. First, just read together. Whether you read a page or read a book, you are making memories and building literacy. Don't overthink this–just squeeze it in as you can and watch reading time quickly become a highlight of your day.

Second, make sure you're discussing what you're reading. This doesn't need to be a formal book report on every book you encounter (please no!) or a tedious question and answer session every evening. Instead, talk as you go:

"How are they feeling now? Why?"
"Do you like his choice? What would you do?"
"What do you think will happen next?"
"It looks like he thinks he is the most important. What's the truth?"
"What was your favorite part of this book?"

With these simple questions you are building emotional intelligence, worldview, logic, observational skills, and so much more.

## Make This List Even Better

We love your book recommendations and feedback! Did you find a book you loved this year? We'd love to add your recommendations! Just shoot us a note at books@timberdoodle.com and let us know. Or, were you perhaps disenchanted with one of our suggestions? Please let us know!

At the end of the year, fill out the Reader Awards on page 119 and submit that. We'll be thrilled to credit you 50 Doodle Dollar Reward points (worth $2.50 off your next order) as our thank you for taking the time to share.

## 1. A BOOK ABOUT BEING A CHRISTIAN OR ABOUT WHAT THE BIBLE TEACHES

*The Ology: Ancient Truths Ever New* by Marty Machowski

*The Biggest Story* by Kevin DeYoung

*The Gospel Story Bible* by Marty Machowski

*Wise Up* by Marty Machowski

*Big Beliefs!* by David R. Helm

*Long Story Short* by Marty Machowski

*Old Story New* by Marty Machowski

*The Garden, the Curtain, and the Cross* by Carl Laferton

*The Tiny Truths Illustrated Bible* by Joanna Rivard and Tim Penner

*Kings and Queens of the Bible* by Mary Hoffman and Christina Balit

## 2. A BOOK ABOUT THE WORLD

*A Ticket Around the World* by Natalia Diaz

*This Is the World* by Miroslav Šašek

*Stories from Around the World* by Heather Amery

*This Is How We Do It* by Matt Lamothe

*DK Pocket Genius: Earth*

*DK Eyewitness: Wonders of the World*

✓ *If the World Were a Village* by David J. Smith

## 3. A BIOGRAPHY

*Harriet Tubman: Conductor on the Underground Railroad* by Ann Petry

*Courageous World Changers: 50 True Stories of Daring Women of God* by Shirley Raye Redmond

*Meet Christopher Columbus* by James T. de Kay

*Who Was?* series

*Mary on Horseback* by Rosemary Wells

*Leif the Lucky* by Ingri and Edgar Parin D'Aulaire

*Easy Reader Biographies* from Scholastic

*Christian Biographies for Young Readers* series by Simonetta Carr

*Heroes of History* series by Janet and Geoff Benge

✓ *Abraham Lincoln* by Ingri and Edgar Parin D'Aulaire

## 4. A CLASSIC NOVEL/STORY

*Little House* series by Laura Ingalls Wilder

*Betsy-Tacy* series by Maud Hart Lovelace

*The Swiss Family Robinson* by Johann David Wyss

✓ *The Voyages of Doctor Dolittle* by Hugh Lofting

*The Chronicles of Narnia* by C.S. Lewis

*The Wind in the Willows* by Kenneth Grahame

## 5. A BOOK YOUR GRANDPARENT (OR OTHER RELATIVE) SAYS WAS HIS/HER FAVORITE AT YOUR AGE

Ask your grandparents or relatives. Or, if that's not possible, ask your Facebook friends for a recommendation for your child.

## 6. A BOOK FROM THE OLD TESTAMENT

This could be a literal book of the Old Testament, or it could be a book based on a section of the Old Testament.

## 7. A BOOK FROM THE NEW TESTAMENT

This could be a literal book of the New Testament, or it could be a book based on a section of the New Testament.

## 8. A BOOK BASED ON A TRUE STORY

✓ *Herbert: The True Story of a Brave Sea Dog* by Robyn Belton
*January's Sparrow* by Patricia Polacco
*The Whispering Town* by Jennifer Elvgren
*Operation Rawhide* by Paul Thomsen
*Bud & Me* by Alta Abernathy
*Keep the Lights Burning, Abbie* by Peter and Connie Roop
*Pocahontas: Princess of Faith and Courage* by Maja Ledgerwood
*The Big Balloon Race* by Eleanor Coerr
*Cora Frear* by Susan E. Goodman
*Riding the Pony Express* by Clyde Robert Bulla
*Brave Girl* by Michelle Markel
*Warm as Wool* by Scott Russell Sanders

## ✓9. A BOOK YOUR PASTOR OR SUNDAY SCHOOL TEACHER RECOMMENDS

Ask your pastor or Sunday School teacher - they will likely be thrilled to share a book they love.

## ✓10. A BOOK MORE THAN 100 YEARS OLD

*Heidi* by Johanna Spyri
*The Secret Garden* by Frances Hodgson Burnett
*A Little Princess* by Frances Hodgson Burnett
*The Wonderful Wizard of Oz* by L. Frank Baum
*Understood Betsy* by Dorothy Canfield Fisher
*Pollyanna* by Eleanor Porter

## 11. A BOOK ABOUT FAMILIES

*The Vanderbeekers to the Rescue* by Karina Yan Glaser
*The Magnificent Mya Tibbs: Mya in the Middle* by Crystal Allen
✓ *Gone Crazy in Alabama* by Rita Williams-Garcia
*The Little Brute Family* by Russell Hoban
*Happy Little Family* by Rebecca Caudill
*The Vanderbeekers of 141st Street* by Karina Yan Glaser
*The Littles* series by John Peterson
*Miracles on Maple Hill* by Virginia Sorensen

*The Long Way to a New Land* by Joan Sandin
*The Long Way Westward* by Joan Sandin
*A Different Pond* by Bao Phi
*Naming Liberty* by Jane Yolen
*Home at Last* by Susan Middleton Elya
*One Green Apple* by Eve Bunting

## 12. A BOOK ABOUT RELATIONSHIPS OR FRIENDSHIP

✓ *Craftily Ever After: The Un-Friendship Bracelet* by Martha Maker
*My Happy Life* by Rose Lagercrantz
*Cul-de-Sac Kids* series by Beverly Lewis
*Betsy and Billy* by Carolyn Haywood
*Jake Drake* series by Andrew Clements
*Friendship According to Humphrey* by Betty G. Birney
*Chester's Way* by Kevin Henkes
*The Blessings of Friendship Treasury* by Mary Engelbreit

## 13. A BOOK FEATURING SOMEONE OF A DIFFERENT ETHNICITY THAN YOU

*The Birchbark House* by Louise Erdrich
*Anna Wang* series by Andrea Cheng
*Betsy and Tacy Go Over the Big Hill* by Maud Hart Lovelace
*Molly's Pilgrim* by Barbara Cohen
✓ *Wagon Wheels* by Barbara Brenner
*Om-kas-toe of the Blackfeet* by Kenneth Thomasma
*Fly High!* by Louise Borden and Mary Kay Kroeger

## 14. A BOOK ABOUT SOMEONE WHO CAME FROM ANOTHER COUNTRY

*Me and Mr. Mah* by Andrea Spalding
*Dreamers* by Yuyi Morales
✓ *All the Way to America* by Dan Yaccarino

## 15. A BOOK OF FAIRY TALES OR FOLK TALES (OR AN EXTENDED RETELLING OF ONE)

*African Folk Tales* by Hugh Vernon-Jackson
✓ *Jack and the Beanstalk* by Steven Kellogg
*The Classic Treasury of Hans Christian Andersen*
*The Candlewick Book of Fairy Tales*
*Grimm's Fairy Tales*
*The King's Equal* by Katherine Paterson
*The Ordinary Princess* by M.M. Kaye
*Fairy Tale Comics* by Chris Duffy
*The Talking Eggs* by Robert D. San Souci

## ✓ 16. A BOOK RECOMMENDED BY A PARENT OR SIBLING

Encourage your child to ask his parents or siblings for a book recommendation. Or, if he prefers to choose his own titles, have him ask for a couple of options from each and let him pick from that list.

## 17. A BOOK BY OR ABOUT A MISSIONARY

*Missionary Stories with the Millers* by Mildred A. Martin
*I Heard Good News Today* by Cornelia Lehn
*Christian Heroes Then and Now* series by Janet and Geoff Benge
*Granny Han's Breakfast* by Sheila Groves
*Hero Tales* by Dave & Neta Jackson
*A Question of Yams* by Gloria Repp

## 19. A BOOK ABOUT A HOLIDAY
*A Charlie Brown Christmas* by Charles M. Schulz
*Andi's Circle C Christmas* by Susan K. Marlow
*Sarah Gives Thanks* by Mike Allegra
*Cranberry* series by Wende Devlin
✓*The Family Under the Bridge* by Natalie Savage Carlson
*The Carpenter's Gift* by David Rubel

## 20. A BOOK ABOUT GRANDPARENTS OR SENIOR CITIZENS
✓*I Am My Grandpa's Enkelin* by Walter Wangerin, Jr.
*Gus and Grandpa* by Claudia Mills
*In Grandma's Attic* by Arleta Richardson
*When Grandmama Sings* by Margaree King Mitchell
*The Canada Geese Quilt* by Natalie Kinsey-Warnock
*Grandfather's Dance* by Patricia MacLachlan
*Tea Cakes for Tosh* by Kelly Starling Lyons

## 21. A BOOK WITH VISUAL PUZZLES
*The Circus Ship* by Chris Van Dusen
*Where's Waldo?* books
✓*I Spy* books
*Usborne 1001 Things to Spot* books
*Disney Look and Find* books
*Highlights Hidden Pictures* books
*Seek and Find Bible Stories* by Carl Anker Mortensen

## 18. A CALDECOTT, NEWBERY, OR GEISEL AWARD WINNER
*The One and Only Ivan* by Katherine Applegate
✓*The Tale of Despereaux* by Kate diCamillo
*Joyful Noise* by Paul Fleischman
*The Whipping Boy* by Sid Fleischman
*So You Want to Be President?* by Judith St. George
*Zelda and Ivy: The Runaways* by Laura McGee Kvasnosky
*Miss Hickory* by Carolyn Sherwin Bailey

## 22. A BOOK THAT HAS A FRUIT IN ITS TITLE
*On the Banks of Plum Creek* by Laura Ingalls Wilder
*Mr. Putter & Tabby Pick the Pears* by Cynthia Rylant
*Johnny Appleseed*
*Little Pear* by Eleanor Frances Lattimore
*How to Make an Apple Pie and See the World* by Marjorie Priceman
✓*How to Make a Cherry Pie and See the U.S.A.* by Marjorie Priceman

## 23. A BOOK ABOUT A FARM

*Farmer Boy* by Laura Ingalls Wilder
*The Clippity-Cloppity Carnival* by Valerie Tripp
*McBroom's Wonderful One-Acre Farm* by Sid Fleischman
*Babe: The Gallant Pig* by Dick King-Smith
*Welcome to Silver Street Farm* by Nicola Davies
*A Farm of Her Own* by Natalie Kinsey-Warnock
*Corn Farm Boy* by Lois Lenski

## 24. A BOOK ABOUT ILLNESS OR MEDICINE

*Sadako and the Thousand Paper Cranes* by Eleanor Coerr
*My Grandpa Had a Stroke* by Dori Hillestad Butler
✓*The Lemonade Club* by Patricia Polacco
*A Doctor Like Papa* by Natalie Kinsey-Warnock
*DK Pocket Genius: Human Body*

## 25. A BOOK ABOUT LEARNING, SCHOOL OR A TEACHER

✓*Steamboat School* by Deborah Hopkinson
*The Magnificent Mya Tibbs: Spirit Week Showdown* by Crystal Allen
*Save Me a Seat* by Sarah Weeks and Gita Varadarajan
*The Wheel on the School* by Meindert DeJong
*Back to School with Betsy* by Carolyn Haywood
*The Year of Miss Agnes* by Kirkpatrick Hill
*Skippack School* by Marguerite De Angeli
*School Days According to Humphrey* by Betty G. Birney
*Sugar Creek Gang: Teacher Trouble* by Paul Hutchens

*Who Was Booker T. Washington?* by James Buckley, Jr.
*Prairie School* by Lois Lenski

## 26. A GRAPHIC NOVEL

✓*Hereville: How Mirka Got Her Sword* by Barry Deutsch
*Pet Shop Private Eye* series by Colleen Venable
*Mr. Badger and Mrs. Fox* series by Brigitte Luciani
*Owly* series by Andy Runton
*Geronimo Stilton* series
*Babymouse* series by Jennifer Holm
Or check our website for other series we love!

## 27. A BOOK OF POETRY

*A Light in the Attic* by Shel Silverstein
✓*The New Kid on the Block* by Jack Prelutsky
*Surprises* by Lee Bennett Hopkins
*The Llama Who Had No Pajama* by Mary Ann Hoberman
*Favorite Poems of Childhood* by Philip Smith
*The Oxford Illustrated Book of American Children's Poems*
*Julie Andrews' Collection of Poems, Songs, and Lullabies*
*Poems to Learn by Heart* by Caroline Kennedy
*Poetry for Young People* series

## 28. A BOOK WITH A GREAT COVER

Let your child choose–it will be interesting to see what he considers to be a great cover!

## 29. A BOOK ABOUT FOOD

✓*The Chocolate Touch* by Patrick Skene Catling
*Fox and Crow Are Not Friends* by Melissa Wiley
*Stick Dog* by Tom Watson
*Tales for Very Picky Eaters* by Josh Schneider
*Holiday Cooking Around the World* compiled by Kari A. Cornell

*Adventures with Waffles* by Maria Parr
*Who Was Julia Child?* by Geoff Edgers and Carlene Hempel

## 30. A BOOK ABOUT WEATHER

✓ *Terrible Storm* by Carol Otis Hurst
*The Littles and the Big Storm* by John Peterson
*The Rainstorm Brainstorm* by Valerie Tripp
*Sugar Creek Gang: One Stormy Day* by Paul Hutchens
*Max Axiom Natural Disasters* graphic novels
*Our Wonderful Weather* by Valerie Bodden
*The Man Who Named the Clouds* by Julie Hanna
*DK Eyewitness: Weather*
*DK Eyewitness: Hurricane & Tornado*
*What Was Hurricane Katrina?* by Robin Koontz
*Flood Friday* by Lois Lenski

## 31. A BOOK ABOUT AN ADVENTURE

*The Adventures of a South Pole Pig* by Chris Kurtz
*Reel Kids Adventures* by Dave Gustaveson
*Lost on a Mountain in Maine* by Donn Fendler
*Peabody Adventure* series by Jeri Massi
*The Bears on Hemlock Mountain* by Alice Dalgliesh
*Mice of the Westing Wind* series by Tim Davis
*The Seven Wonders of Sassafras Springs* by Betty G. Birney
*Spy Mice* series by Heather Vogel Frederick

## 32. A BOOK BY OR ABOUT WILLIAM SHAKESPEARE

✓ *A Stage Full of Shakespeare Stories* by Angela McAllister
*Graphic Shakespeare*
*Bard of Avon* by Diane Stanley
*William Shakespeare and the Globe* by Aliki
*Will's Words* by Jane Sutcliffe
*Mr. William Shakespeare's Plays* by Marcia Williams
*Usborne Illustrated Stories from Shakespeare*

## 33. A FUNNY BOOK

*Paul Bunyan* by Steven Kellogg
*Pippi Longstocking* by Astrid Lindgren
*Mercy Watson* series by Kate DiCamillo
*Freddy Goes to Florida* and others by Walter R. Brooks
*Mr. Popper's Penguins* by Richard and Florence Atwater
*Mrs. Piggle-Wiggle* series by Betty MacDonald
*Knock-Knock Jokes For Kids* by Rob Elliott

## 34. A MYSTERY OR DETECTIVE STORY

*A to Z Mysteries* series by Ron Roy
✓ *The Boxcar Children* series by Gertrude Chandler Warner
*The Happy Hollisters* series by Jerry West
*The Bobbsey Twins* series by Laura Lee Hope
*Red Rock Mysteries* series by Jerry B. Jenkins and Chris Fabry
*Third-Grade Detectives* series by George E. Stanley
*J.J. Tully* series by Doreen Cronin
*The Crime-Solving Cousins* series by Shannon L. Brown

## 35. A PICTURE BOOK

Choose one of your favorite picture books to re-read, or choose one you've never read before that appeals to you.

## 36. A BOOK BY OR ABOUT A FAMOUS AMERICAN

*Childhood of Famous Americans* series
*Rutherford B., Who Was He?: Poems About Our Presidents* by Marilyn Singer
✓*The President's Stuck in the Bathtub* by Susan Katz
*Meet George Washington* by Joan Heilbroner
*Meet Thomas Jefferson* by Marvin Barrett
*Meet Abraham Lincoln* by Barbara Cary
*Ben and Me* by Robert Lawson
*DK Eyewitness: First Ladies*
*DK Eyewitness: Presidents*
*A Place to Land* by Barry Wittenstein

## 37. A BOOK ABOUT THE RENAISSANCE

*Good Queen Bess* by Diane Stanley
*Leonardo da Vinci* by Diane Stanley
• *Marguerite Makes a Book* by Bruce Robertson
*Leonardo da Vinci for Kids* by Janis Herbert
*Galileo for Kids* by Richard Panchyk
*Michelangelo for Kids* by Simonetta Carr

## 38. A BOOK ABOUT EARLY AMERICAN HISTORY

*A Spy Called James* by Anne Rockwell
✓*A Kid's Guide to Native American History* by Yvonne Wakim Dennis and Arlene Hirschfelder
*The Courage of Sarah Noble* by Alice Dalgliesh
*Mr. Revere and I* by Robert Lawson
*The Secret Valley* by Clyde Robert Bulla
*Johnny Tremain* by Esther Forbes
*The Arrow over the Door* by Joseph Bruchac
*Finding Providence* by Avi
*George vs. George* by Rosalyn Schanzer
*DK Eyewitness: American Revolution*

## 39. A BOOK ABOUT MONEY

✓*The Toothpaste Millionaire* by Jean Merrill
*Sled Dog School* by Terry Lynn Johnson
*Lawn Boy* by Gary Paulsen
*Show Me the Money* by Alvin Hall
*Sugar Creek Gang: Thousand Dollar Fish* by Paul Hutchens
*The Tuttle Twins and the Food Truck Fiasco* by Connor Boyack
*Fox on the Job* by James Marshall
*Shoeshine Girl* by Clyde Robert Bulla
*DK Eyewitness: Money*

## ✓40. A BOOK ABOUT ART OR ARTISTS

*A Dance Like Starlight* by Kristy Dempsey
*Katie* series by James Mayhew
*Famous Children* series by Tony Hart
*Getting to Know the World's Greatest Artists* series by Mike Venezia
*Artists Books for Children* series by Laurence Anholt
*How Artists See* series by Colleen Carroll
*The Chalk Box Kid* by Clyde Robert Bulla
*The Paint Brush Kid* by Clyde Robert Bulla
*The Boy Who Drew Birds* by Jacqueline Davies
FREIDA

*The Inventor's Secret* by Suzanne Slade
*The Kid Who Invented the Popsicle* by Don L. Wulffson
*Ben Franklin's Big Splash* by Barb Rosenstock
*DK Eyewitness: Invention*

## 43. A BOOK OF CRAFTS OR GAMES
*101 Ways to Amaze & Entertain* by Peter Gross
· *Sidewalk Chalk* by Jamie Kyle McGillian
*Cat's Cradle* by Anne Akers Johnson
*Juggling for the Complete Klutz* by John Cassidy and B.C. Rimbeaux
*Low-Mess Crafts for Kids* by Debbie Chapman
*A Kid's Guide to Awesome Duct Tape Projects* by Instructables.com
*101 Things to Do Outside* from Weldon Owen

## 44. A BOOK ABOUT A BOY
· *Henry Huggins* series by Beverly Cleary
*Homer Price* by Robert McCloskey
*Goldtown Adventures* series by Susan K. Marlow
*EllRay Jakes* series by Sally Warner
*Flat Stanley* by Jeff Brown
*Billy and Blaze* series by C.W. Anderson
*San Francisco Boy* by Lois Lenski
*Harry Miller's Run* by David Almond

## ✓45. A BOOK ABOUT A GIRL
*Melody: Never Stop Singing* by Denise Lewis Patrick
*American Girl* series
*Strawberry Girl* by Lois Lenski
*Bayou Suzette* by Lois Lenski
*Ramona* books by Beverly Cleary
· *Emily's Runaway Imagination* by Beverly Cleary
*Ruthie's Gift* by Kimberly Brubaker Bradley
*Phoebe the Spy* by Judith Berry Griffin

## 41. A BOOK ABOUT MUSIC OR A MUSICIAN
*Soldier Song* by Debbie Levy
✓*Swing Sisters* by Karen Deans
*This Jazz Man* by Karen Ehrhardt
*Melody: No Ordinary Sound* by Denise Lewis Patrick
*Composer* series by Anna Harwell Celenza
*A Band of Angels* by Deborah Hopkinson
*Mr. Putter & Tabby Toot the Horn* by Cynthia Rylant
*Hana Hashimoto, Sixth Violin* by Chieri Uegaki
*Who Was Wolfgang Amadeus Mozart?* by Yona Zeldis McDonough
*Blue Ridge Billy* by Lois Lenski

## 42. A BOOK ABOUT AN INVENTION OR INVENTOR
*A Weed Is a Flower* by Aliki
*Inventions and Discovery* set (*Graphic Library*)
*Robert Fulton: Boy Craftsman* by Marguerite Henry
*How Things Are Made* by Oldrich Ruzicka
· *The Boo-Boos That Changed the World* by Barry Wittenstein
*Electrical Wizard* by Elizabeth Rusch

37) ~~MARGUERITE BOOK~~
45) ~~AMERICAN GIRL~~
40) ~~FRIDAY~~
46) ~~BOB THE ALIEN~~
47) PENNY & PETER
48) ~~SONG WHALE~~
50) ONCE UPON A BABY BROTHER
51) RIGHT WORD
52.) RESCUERS
53.) WHAT EVERY CHILD SHOULD KNOW
54.) ~~LASSIE~~

### 46. A BOOK ABOUT BOOKS OR A LIBRARY

*Schomburg: The Man Who Built a Library* by Carole Bo Weatherford
*Lumber Camp Library* by Natalie Kinsey-Warnock
*The Tiny Hero of Ferny Creek Library* by Linda Bailey
*Clara and the Bookwagon* by Nancy Smiler Levinson
*Mr. Putter & Tabby Turn the Page* by Cynthia Rylant
*The Year of the Book* by Andrea Cheng
*Absolutely Truly* by Heather Vogel Frederick
*That Book Woman* by Heather Henson
*Karl and Carolina Uncover the Parts of a Book* by Sanc Donovan
• *Bob the Alien Discovers the Dewey Decimal System* by Donovan
*A Book Is Just Like You!* by Kathleen Fox

### 47. A BOOK ABOUT ADOPTION

*Penny and Peter* by Carolyn Haywood
*Here's a Penny* by Carolyn Haywood
*All About Adoption* by Marc Nemiroff and Jane Annunziata
*At Home in This World* by Jean MacLeod
*Three Names of Me* by Mary Cummings

### 48. A BOOK ABOUT SOMEONE WHO IS DIFFERENTLY ABLED

• *Song for a Whale* by Lynne Kelly
*Rescue and Jessica* by Jessica Kensky and Patrick Downes
*A Splash of Red* by Jen Bryant
*A Boy and a Jaguar* by Alan Rabinowitz
*My Brother Charlie* by Holly Robinson Peete and Ryan Elizabeth Peete
*Helen's Big World* by Doreen Rappaport
*Annie and Helen* by Deborah Hopkinson and Raul Colón

### ... OWNS BUT

... read every book in ... ve walked past at the ... people talking about

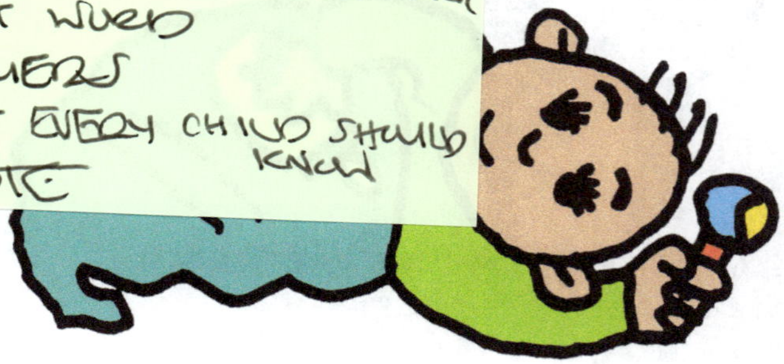

### 50. A BOOK ABOUT BABIES

*The Year of the Baby* by Andrea Cheng
*Betsy's Little Star* by Carolyn Haywood
*Once Upon a Baby Brother* by Sarah Sullivan
*Lavender* by Karen Hesse
*Cam Jansen and the Valentine Baby Mystery* by David Adler
*Iris and Walter and Baby Rose* by Elissa Haden Guest
*Hank Zipzer: Who Ordered This Baby? Definitely Not Me!* by Henry Winkler and Lin Oliver
*Here We All Are* by Tomie DePaola

### 51. A BOOK ABOUT WRITING

*Mr. Putter & Tabby Write the Book* by Cynthia Rylant
*The Right Word: Roget and His Thesaurus* by Jen Bryant
*Nancy Clancy: Late-Breaking News!* by Jane O'Connor
*Home Work* by Arthur Yorinks

*Ralph Tells a Story* by Abby Hanlon
*The Best Story* by Eileen Spinelli
*Little Red Writing* by Joan Holub
*What Do Authors Do?* by Eileen Christelow
*Chips and Cheese and Nana's Knees* by Brian P. Cleary
*A Bat Cannot Bat, a Stair Cannot Stare* by Brian P. Cleary
*Quirky, Jerky, Extra Perky* by Brian P. Cleary
*Hero Dog* by Hilde Lysiak

## 52. A BOOK MADE INTO A MOVIE
*Charlotte's Web* by E.B. White
*Cloudy with a Chance of Meatballs* by Judi Barrett
*A Bear Called Paddington* by Michael Bond
*Meet Felicity: An American Girl* by Valerie Tripp
*The Rescuers* by Margery Sharp

## 53. A BOOK ABOUT PRAYER
*What Every Child Should Know About Prayer* by Nancy
   Guthrie
*From Akebu to Zapotec* by June Hathersmith
*Asking Father* by E. & L. Harvey and Trudy Tait
*Window on the World* from Operation World

## ✓54. A BOOK RECOMMENDED BY A LIBRARIAN OR TEACHER
Ask your librarian, ballet teacher, karate instructor, Sunday
School teacher...

## 55. AN ENCYCLOPEDIA, DICTIONARY, OR ALMANAC
This is unlikely to be a book you'll read cover-to-cover, yet
it's definitely a resource you want your child to be familiar
with. Consider reading a set number of pages or spending a
specified amount of time and then checking it off the list.

*The Usborne Children's Encyclopedia*
*The Usborne Encyclopedia of Planet Earth*

*Scholastic Children's Encyclopedia*
*DK Smithsonian Picturepedia*
*DK Merriam-Webster's Children's Dictionary*
*Record-Breaking People* by John Richards and Ed Simkins

## 56. A BOOK ABOUT BUILDING OR ARCHITECTURE
*Fallingwater* by Marc Harshman & Anna Egan Smucker
*How Emily Saved the Bridge* by Frieda Wishinsky
*Skyscrapers! Super Structures* by Carol Johnman
*Roberto: The Insect Architect* by Nina Laden
*Architecture According to Pigeons* by Speck Lee Tailfeather
*Angelo* by David Macaulay
*How Do Dams Work?* by Ryan Nagelhout

### 57. A BIOGRAPHY OF A WORLD LEADER

*Peter the Great* by Diane Stanley
*To Dare Mighty Things: The Life of Theodore Roosevelt* by
    Doreen Rappaport
*My Brother Martin* by Christine King Farris
*Who Was Nelson Mandela?* by Pam Pollack and Meg Belviso
*DK Eyewitness: Gandhi*
*William Wilberforce: Take Up the Fight* by Janet and Geoff
    Benge

### 58. A BOOK PUBLISHED THE SAME YEAR YOUR THIRD-GRADER WAS BORN

You choose. Stumped? We found that searching for "best childrens' books of 20 ___" provided several lists to browse.

### 59. A BOOK WITH A ONE-WORD TITLE

*Frindle* by Andrew Clements
*Tornado* by Betsy Byars
*Begin* by Philip Ulrich

### 60. A BOOK OR MAGAZINE ABOUT A CAREER YOU'RE INTERESTED IN

Ask someone in that career for recommendations.

### 61. A BOOK ABOUT SIBLINGS

*Treasure Hunters* series by James Patterson and Chris Grabenstein
*Beezus and Ramona* by Beverly Cleary
*Beyond the Orphan Train* series by Arleta Richardson
*Ling and Ting* series by Grace Lin
*The Penderwicks* series by Jeanne Birdsall

### 62. A BOOK ABOUT ANIMALS

*Sparky!* by Jenny Offill
*Heartwood Hotel: A True Home* by Kallie George
*Capyboppy* by Bill Peet
*Rabbit Hill* by Robert Lawson
*Mountain Born* by Elizabeth Yates
*Lulu* series by Hilary McKay
*Owls in the Family* by Farley Mowat
*Gentle Ben* by Walt Morey

### 63. A BOOK FEATURING A DOG

*Absolutely Lucy* by Ilene Cooper
*Barkus* by Patricia MacLauchlan
*Tippy Lemmey* by Patricia C. McKissack
*Along Came a Dog* by Meindert DeJong
*Five True Dog Stories* by Margaret Davidson
*Dogku* by Andrew Clements
*DK Eyewitness: Dog*
*Ribsy* by Beverly Cleary

### 64. A BOOK FEATURING A HORSE

*Sergeant Reckless* by Patricia McCormick
*Step Right Up* by Donna Janell Bowman
*Pony Pals* series by Jeanne Betancourt
*The Black Stallion* series by Walter Farley
*Misty of Chincoteague* and others by Marguerite Henry
*My Friend Flicka* by Mary O'Hara
*Who Was Seabiscuit?* by James Buckley, Jr.
*DK Pocket Genius: Horses*

## 65. A BOOK YOU HAVE STARTED BUT NEVER FINISHED
You choose!

## 66. A BOOK ABOUT PLANTS OR GARDENING
*The Friendship Garden* series by Jenny Meyerhoff
*The Vanderbeekers and the Hidden Garden* by Karina Yan Glaser
*The Year of the Garden* by Andrea Cheng
*Usborne Gardening for Beginners*
*Me and the Pumpkin Queen* by Marlane Kennedy

## 67. A BOOK ABOUT A HOBBY OR A SKILL YOU WANT TO LEARN
You choose! Is there something that your child would enjoy learning? From science experiments to building a fort, there's a book for everything. Keep in mind that the skill doesn't have to be feasible to use right away. Choosing a horse or flying a spaceship are fair game!

## 68. A BOOK OF COMICS
*Peanuts* by Charles Schulz
*Family Circus* by Bil Keane
*Calvin and Hobbes* by Bill Watterson
*The Adventures of Tintin* by Hergé
*Red and Rover* by Brian Basset

## 69. A BOOK ABOUT A FAMOUS WAR
*You Can Fly* by Carole Boston Weatherford
*Pink and Say* by Patricia Polacco
*True Stories of War* graphic novels
*Primrose Day* by Carolyn Haywood
*Twenty and Ten* by Claire Huchet Bishop
*The Perilous Road* by William O. Steele
*Shades of Gray* by Carolyn Reeder
*Across the Blue Pacific* by Louise Borden
*Welcome to Molly's World* by Catherine Gourley
*Civil War Sub* by Kate Boehm Jerome

## 70. A BOOK ABOUT SPORTS
*We Are the Ship* by Kadir Nelson
*Just Jump!* by Mabel Elizabeth Singletary
*Something to Prove* by Rob Skead
*Mr. Putter & Tabby Drop the Ball* by Cynthia Rylant
*Betsy and the Boys* by Carolyn Haywood
*Brothers at Bat* by Audrey Vernick
*Mighty Jackie* by Marissa Moss
*Dugout Rivals* by Fred Bowen
*The Zach & Zoe Mysteries* series by Mike Lupica
*DK Eyewitness: Baseball*

## 71. A BOOK ABOUT MATH

*Ben Franklin and the Magic Squares* by Frank Murphy
*Life of Fred* series
*A Hundred Billion Trillion Stars* by Seth Fishman
*Mystery Math* by David A. Adler
*Sir Cumference* series by Cindy Neuschwander
*The Lion's Share* by Matthew McElligott
*One Grain of Rice* by Demi
*Go Figure!* by Johnny Ball
*How Many Guinea Pigs Can Fit on a Plane?* by Laura Overdeck

## 72. A BOOK ABOUT SUFFERING OR POVERTY

*The Hundred Dresses* by Eleanor Estes
*Henry's Freedom Box* by Ellen Levine
*Esperanza Rising* by Pam Muñoz Ryan
*A Letter to Mrs. Roosevelt* by C. Coco De Young
*Blue Willow* by Doris Gates
*Only the Names Remain* by Alex W. Bealer
*If Wishes Were Horses* by Natalie Kinsey-Warnock
*What Was the Great Depression?* by Janet B. Pascal
*Mama Hattie's Girl* by Lois Lenski

## 73. A BOOK BY YOUR FAVORITE AUTHOR

Your child will choose this one, though you may have to help him think through his favorite books to narrow down the author he's enjoying most right now.

## 74. A BOOK YOU'VE READ BEFORE

Your child should choose, and make sure you mark it down, since it's obviously one he finds interesting!

## 75. A BOOK WITH AN UGLY COVER

Let your child choose, of course, and make sure to document what he thinks is ugly about it!

## 76. A CHRISTIAN NOVEL

*Circle C Beginnings* novels by Susan K. Marlow
*The Adventures of Adam Raccoon* by Glen Keane
*Sugar Creek Gang* series by Paul Hutchens
*Imagination Station* series by Adventures in Odyssey
*The Prince Warriors* series by Priscilla Shirer
*The Scripture Sleuth* series by Mat Halverson

## 77. A BOOK ABOUT TRAVEL OR TRANSPORTATION

*Mercy Watson Goes for a Ride* by Kate DiCamillo
*National Geographic Kids Ultimate U.S. Road Trip Atlas*
*LaRue Across America* by Mark Teague
*Arthur's Family Vacation* by Marc Brown
*On the Road* by Lucy Nolan
*DK Eyewitness: Car*
*DK Eyewitness: Train*
*Wagons Ho!* by George Hallowell and Joan Holub
*Judy's Journey* by Lois Lenski

## 78. A BOOK ABOUT THE NATURAL WORLD

*Crinkleroot's Guide* series by Jim Arnosky
*Willa's Wilderness Campout* by Valerie Tripp

*Nature Anatomy* by Julia Rothman
*Pony Scouts: The Camping Trip* by Catherine Hapka
*A Week in the Woods* by Andrew Clements
*Fins, Feathers, and Faith: Wisdom from God's Amazing Creation*
     by William L. Coleman
*The Work of Thy Fingers* by Pablo Yoder
*Out of Sight* by Seymour Simon

## 79. A BIOGRAPHY OF AN AUTHOR
*Big Machines: The Story of Virginia Lee Burton* by Sherri
     Duskey Rinker
*Just Like Beverly* by Vicki Conrad
*A Boy, a Mouse, and a Spider--The Story of E. B. White* by
     Barbara Herkert
*John Ronald's Dragons: The Story of J. R. R. Tolkien* by Caroline
     McAlister
*Noah Webster's Fighting Words* by Tracy Nelson Maurer
*Ordinary, Extraordinary Jane Austen* by Deborah Hopkinson
*C.S. Lewis: Master Storyteller* by Janet and Geoff Benge

## 80. A BOOK PUBLISHED IN 2020-2021
Your librarian should be able to point you towards the
new releases that are age-appropriate (you may want to
preview them, though!) or you can watch to see what's being
featured in your favorite book-seller's email or storefront.
Of course, you could also expand this category to be any
brand-new book or new-to-your-library title.

## 81. A HISTORICAL FICTION BOOK
*All Different Now* by Angela Johnson
*Magic Tree House* series by Mary Pope Osborne
*Thee, Hannah!* by Marguerite de Angeli
*Clipper Ship* by Thomas P. Lewis
*Sam the Minuteman* by Nathaniel Benchley
*Prairie Friends* by Nancy Smiler Levinson

*Daniel's Duck* by Clyde Robert Bulla
*Caddie Woodlawn* by Carol Ryrie Brink

## 82. A BOOK ABOUT SCIENCE OR A SCIENTIST
*Indescribable* by Louie Giglio
*Wile E. Coyote Physical Science Genius* series
*Max Axiom* graphic novels
*Superman Science* by Agnieszka Biskup
*Wells of Knowledge Science* series
*I, Galileo* by Bonnie Christensen
*DK Eyewitness: Science*
*Solving the Puzzle Under the Sea* by Robert Burleigh
*Magnets Push, Magnets Pull* by Mark Weakland
*Chemistry: The Atom and Elements* by April Chloe Terrazas
*Amber's Atoms* by E.M. Robinson

### 83. A BOOK ABOUT SAFETY OR SURVIVAL

Do your kids know both when and how to call 911? As landlines become less common, you will want to make sure that your child knows how to access 911 on the actual devices he has access to every day. You won't see that specifically addressed in these books, but it is worth setting some time aside to discuss this with your child. (BTW, if you accidentally actually dial 911, stay on the line. Every department is different, but here our police department is obligated to investigate every 911 hang-up for obvious reasons. If you stay on the line and explain, that will save everyone some time.)

This is also a great opportunity to visit your local fire and police departments for a tour. Your child will learn a ton about his community, and they often have helpful handouts– for instance, fire escape planning info, etc.

*Kids to the Rescue!* by Maribeth Boelts
*Titan and the Wild Boars: The True Cave Rescue of the Thai Soccer Team* by Susan Hood and Pathana Sornhiran
*The SOS File* by Betsy Byars, Betsy Duffey, and Laurie Myers
*I Survived* series by Lauren Tarshis
*First Aid Basics* by Elizabeth Lang

### 84. A BOOK ABOUT SPACE OR AN ASTRONAUT

*Mr. Putter & Tabby See the Stars* by Cynthia Rylant
*Mae Among the Stars* by Roda Ahmed
*Caroline's Comets* by Emily Arnold McCully
*DK Pocket Genius: Space*
*DK Eyewitness: Astronomy*
*The Challenger Explosion* by Heather Adamson
*Reaching for the Moon* by Buzz Aldrin
*Neil Armstrong: Young Flyer* by Montrew Dunham
*The Solar System* by Howard K. Trammel
*The Moon Over Star* by Dianna Hutts Aston

### 85. A BOOK SET IN CENTRAL OR SOUTH AMERICA

*A Kid's Guide to Latino History* by Valerie Petrillo
*Hill of Fire* by Thomas P. Lewis
*A Bear for Miguel* by Elaine Marie Alphin
*Secret of the Andes* by Ann Nolan Clark

*The Corn Grows Ripe* by Dorothy Rhoads
*The Dragon Slayer* by Jaime Hernandez
*Ada's Violin* by Susan Hood
*Love and Roast Chicken* by Barbara Knutson
*The Amazing Mexican Secret* by Jeff Brown and Macky
    Pamintuan
*Where Is Machu Picchu?* by Megan Stine

## 86. A BOOK SET IN AFRICA
*The Water Princess* by Susan Verde
*Anna Hibiscus* series by Atinuke
*Beat the Story-Drum, Pum-Pum* by Ashley Bryan
*Mama Miti* by Donna Jo Napoli
*Mufaro's Beautiful Daughters* by John Steptoe
*The African Safari Discovery* by Jeff Brown and Macky
    Pamintuan
*David Livingstone: Africa's Trailblazer* by Janet and Geoff
    Benge
*A Girl Named Disaster* by Nancy Farmer

## 87. A BOOK SET IN ASIA
*Tiger Boy* by Mitali Perkins
*Little One-Inch and Other Japanese Children's Favorite Stories*
    compiled by Florence Sakade
*Evie and Andrew's Asian Adventures in Taiwan* by Katie Do
    Guthrie
*Ruby's Wish* by Shirin Yim Bridges
*Mei Fuh: Memories from China* by Edith Schaeffer
*The Land I Lost* by Quang Nhuong Huynh
*Tikki Tikki Tembo* by Arlene Mosel
*A Grain of Rice* by Helena Clare Pittman
*The Flying Chinese Wonders* by Jeff Brown and Macky
    Pamintuan
*Where Is the Great Wall?* by Patricia Brennan Demuth
*Hudson Taylor: Deep in the Heart of China* by Janet and Geoff
    Benge

*India* by A. Kamala Dalal

## 88. A BOOK SET IN EUROPE
*George Müller: The Guardian of Bristol's Orphans* by Janet and
    Geoff Benge
*White Stallion of Lipizza* by Marguerite Henry
*The Martha Years* series by Melissa Wiley
*The House on Walenska Street* by Charlotte Herman
*Framed in France* by Jeff Brown and Macky Pamintuan
*Count Your Way Through France* by Jim Haskins and Kathleen
    Benson
*Netherlands* by Julie Murray

## 89. A BOOK WITH A COLOR IN ITS TITLE

*The Case of the Weird Blue Chicken* by Doreen Cronin
*The Red Fairy Book* and others by Andrew Lang
*The Yellow House Mystery* by Gertrude Chandler Warner
*Blue Bay Mystery* by Gertrude Chandler Warner
*Encyclopedia Brown* series by Donald J. Sobol
*Sugar Creek Gang: The Green Tent Mystery* by Paul Hutchens
*The Green Glass Sea* by Ellen Klages
*The Green Ember* series by S.D. Smith

## 90. A BOOK ABOUT MANNERS

*Dear Mr. Washington* by Lynn Cullen
*Emily Post's The Guide to Good Manners for Kids*
*A Kid's Guide to Manners* by Katherine Flannery

## 91. A BOOK ABOUT SPRING

*Spring According to Humphrey* by Betty G. Birney
*The Riddle of the Robin* by Valerie Tripp
*The Penderwicks in Spring* by Jeanne Birdsall
*When Spring Comes* by Kevin Henkes
*Mud Flat April Fool* by James Stevenson
*Robins! How They Grow Up* by Eileen Christelow

## 92. A BOOK ABOUT SUMMER

*One Crazy Summer* by Rita Williams-Garcia
*A Promise and a Rainbow* by Mabel Elizabeth Singletary
*Andi's Indian Summer* by Susan K. Marlow
*Summer According to Humphrey* by Betty G. Birney
*Thimble Summer* by Elizabeth Enright
*Ice Cream Summer* by Peter Sis
*The Penderwicks: A Summer Tale...* by Jeanne Birdsall
*Love, Ruby Lavender* by Deborah Wiles
*Houseboat Girl* by Lois Lenski
*Surprise Island* by Gertrude Chandler Warner

## 93. A BOOK ABOUT AUTUMN

*The Friendship Garden: Pumpkin Spice* by Jenny Meyerhoff
*The Muddily-Puddily Show* by Valerie Tripp
*Apple Cider-Making Days* by Ann Purmell
*If You Were at the First Thanksgiving* by Anne Kamma

## 94. A BOOK ABOUT WINTER

*Pugs of the Frozen North* by Philip Reeve
*Bear and Wolf* by Daniel Salmieri
*The Mystery of Mr. E* by Valerie Tripp
*The Happy Hollisters at Snowflake Camp* by Jerry West
*Winter According to Humphrey* by Betty G. Birney
*Sugar Creek Gang: The Winter Rescue* by Paul Hutchens
*The Smallest Snowflake* by Bernadette Watts
*Snowbound Mystery* by Gertrude Chandler Warner

**95. A BOOK FROM THE 000-099 DEWEY DECIMAL SECTION OF YOUR LIBRARY**

Books about computer science, information, and general works

**96. A BOOK FROM THE 100-199 DEWEY DECIMAL SECTION OF YOUR LIBRARY**

Books about philosophy and psychology

**97. A BOOK FROM THE 200-299 DEWEY DECIMAL SECTION OF YOUR LIBRARY**

Books about religion

**98. A BOOK FROM THE 300-399 DEWEY DECIMAL SECTION OF YOUR LIBRARY**

Books about social sciences

**99. A BOOK FROM THE 400-499 DEWEY DECIMAL SECTION OF YOUR LIBRARY**

Books about language

**100. A BOOK FROM THE 500-599 DEWEY DECIMAL SECTION OF YOUR LIBRARY**

Books about science

**101. A BOOK FROM THE 600-699 DEWEY DECIMAL SECTION OF YOUR LIBRARY**

Books about technology

**102. A BOOK FROM THE 700-799 DEWEY DECIMAL SECTION OF YOUR LIBRARY**

Books about arts and recreation

**103. A BOOK FROM THE 800-899 DEWEY DECIMAL SECTION OF YOUR LIBRARY**

Books about literature

**104. A BOOK FROM THE 900-999 DEWEY DECIMAL SECTION OF YOUR LIBRARY**

Books about history and geography

# BOOK AWARDS & PARTY!

## DO THIS AS SOON AS YOU FINISH YOUR READING CHALLENGE!

Grab your child's reading list from pages 30-35 and help him fill out the awards page (opposite page) to give his best and worst books an official award and mark them as most memorable this year.

Encourage him not to agonize over "was this one really the best..." but to go with his general impressions or write down all the contenders.

Send us a copy of this at books@timberdoodle.com and we'll be thrilled to credit you 50 Doodle Dollar Reward points (worth $2.50 off your next order) as our thank you for taking the time to share. We'll also congratulate your child on a job so well done!

**Bonus Idea**

Have an "awards ceremony" night all about one of the books on your list! You'll get the most specific ideas by searching online for "*book I picked* theme party," but here are some things to think through as you get started.

Food: How can you tie the menu to the theme? A book like Green Eggs and Ham or Pancakes for Breakfast is easy–just replicate the food in the book! If you're working with a book that doesn't feature food directly, there are a few options. Perhaps the book featured a construction crew; you could all eat from "lunchboxes" tonight or set up your kitchen to masquerade as a food truck. Or, if you're reading a book about the pioneers, do a little research and eat frying pan bread, beans, venison, and cornmeal mush.

You could also take the food you would normally eat and reshape it to match your story. For instance, sandwiches can be cut into ships, round apple slices can be life preservers, crackers can be labeled "hard tack," and you're well on your way to a party featuring your favorite nautical tale.

Don't forget the setting, too. As ridiculous as it sounds, eating dinner by (battery-operated!) lantern light under your table draped with blankets will make that simple camping tale an experience your family will be recalling for years to come.

Or perhaps some handmade red table fans, softly playing traditional Chinese music, and a red tablecloth would provide the perfect backdrop for the story about life in China.

The more senses you use, the more memorable you make this experience. Use appropriate background music, diffuse peppermint oil to make it smell like Christmas, dim the lights, eat at the top of the playground, or whatever would set this apart from a regular night and make it just a bit crazy and fun.

Don't get trapped in either the "we must do this tonight" mode or in the "we can't do this because it won't be perfect" mode. Allowing your child to spend a few days creating decorations and menus is wonderful! Doing it today because it's the only free night on the horizon even though you can only integrate a few ideas into the preset menu? Also amazing! Your goal is to value the book and make some fun memories.

# BOOK AWARDS OF

(YOUR CHILD'S NAME HERE ^)                                    (YEAR HERE ^)

I READ _____ BOOKS FROM THE READING CHALLENGE THIS YEAR!

FUNNIEST BOOK:

MOST MEMORABLE BOOK:

BOOK I READ THE MOST TIMES:

BOOK I ENJOYED LEAST:

TEACHER'S FAVORITE BOOK:

BOOK I MOST WISH WAS A SERIES:

CHOOSE YOUR OWN AWARD:

# YOUR TOP 4 FAQ ABOUT NEXT YEAR

## THINGS TO THINK THROUGH AS YOU ANTICIPATE FOURTH GRADE

So, you're finishing up third grade already? How has it gone for you? Really, we'd love to know! (Plus, you get reward points for your review.) Just jump over to the Third-Grade Curriculum on our website and scroll down to submit a review.

As you look towards next year, there are a few things that you may want to know.

### 1. When Can We See the New Kits?

New kits usually release in April. Check our Facebook or give us a call for this year's projection, but it's always in the spring and usually April. Each year discontinued items are replaced, and any spectacular new items are added. It is rare to change significant parts of the scope and sequence for a grade, but it's common to add little bits of "wow" that we've been busy all year finding.

### 2. Free Customization

If your child has raced ahead in some subjects this year, or if you've realized you need to go back and fill in some gaps, or if you simply don't need more Math-U-See blocks, you'll be thrilled to know that you can customize your kit next year to accommodate that. You'll find full details on our website, but know that it is free and can often be completed online if you prefer to DIY.

### 3. Do I Need to Take the Summer Off?

Some students finish the grade with an eager passion to jump right into the next grade, and parents contact us asking if that's really okay or if they should take some time off so the child doesn't burn out. We are year-round homeschoolers, so we would definitely be fans of jumping into the next grade here!

However, the truth is that this is a decision only you can make. We can tell you that a long break can quench the thirst for knowledge, so if it were our child, we'd seriously consider moving right into the next grade. However, sometimes a little suspense makes the year begin with a beautiful anticipation!

If you decide to start early, you could consider saving one or two items for your official start date so that there is still some anticipation.

### 4. Can I Refill This Kit for My Next Child?

Absolutely! Each year's Additional Student Kit reflects the current year's kit (so the 2020-2021 Third-Grade Elite Kit and the 2020–2021 Additional Student Kit correlate). If you loved it just the way it was, refill it now before we swap things around for next year. Or, if you prefer, wait for the new kits to launch and then let our team help you figure out what tweaks (if any) need to be made to the standard Additional Student Kit.

### We're Here to Help!

If you have other questions for us, would like to share additional feedback, or would like to get in touch for some other reason, don't hesitate to drop us a line or give us a call. (FYI, we also have online chat on our website, if that's easier for you.)

mail@Timberdoodle.com
800-478-0672
360-426-0672

# DOODLE DOLLAR REWARD POINTS

## WHAT THEY ARE, HOW THEY WORK, AND WHERE TO FIND THEM

*If you're one of our Charter School BFFs, we just want to give you a heads up that the following information doesn't really apply to you. Doodle Dollars are earned on individual prepaid orders (credit cards or online payment plans are fine) and don't apply to purchase orders or school district orders. Sorry about that!*

Now, with that out of the way, here's the good news. Almost any item you order directly from us earns you reward points! You will earn 1 point for every $1 you spend. 20 points = $1 off a future order!

Some families prefer to use this money as they go, while others save it up for Christmas or for those mid-year purchases that just weren't in the budget.

### Can I Earn More Points?
Absolutely! Review your purchases on Timberdoodle.com to earn points. Add pictures for even more points!

We also usually have a few reward point events throughout the year, as well as our year-round Doodle Crew opportunities.

### What Can I Spend My Points On?
Anything on our website. These reward points act as a gift certificate to be used on anything you like.

### How Do I Get to My Points?
The simplest way is to scroll down to the bottom of our website and look for the Doodle Dollars link, listed under Account. If you run into any challenges, please let our team know and we will be thrilled to assist you.

Check our website for the latest information on reward points:
www.Timberdoodle.com/doodledollars